PLANNING
YOUR
DISSERTATION

POCKET STUDY SKILLS

*Series Editor: **Kate Williams**, Oxford Brookes University, UK*
Illustrations by Sallie Godwin

For the time-pushed student, the *Pocket Study Skills* pack a lot of advice into a little book. Each guide focuses on a single crucial aspect of study giving you step-by-step guidance, handy tips and clear advice on how to approach the important areas which will continually be at the core of your studies.

Published

14 Days to Exam Success (2nd edn)
Analyzing a Case Study
Brilliant Writing Tips for Students
Completing Your PhD
Doing Research (2nd edn)
Getting Critical (2nd edn)
Managing Stress
Planning Your Dissertation (2nd edn)
Planning Your Essay (2nd edn)
Planning Your PhD
Posters and Presentations

Reading and Making Notes (2nd edn)
Referencing and Understanding Plagiarism (2nd edn)
Reflective Writing
Report Writing (2nd edn)
Science Study Skills
Studying with Dyslexia (2nd edn)
Success in Groupwork
Time Management
Where's Your Argument?
Writing for University (2nd edn)

POCKET STUDY SKILLS

Kate Williams

PLANNING YOUR DISSERTATION

SECOND EDITION

macmillan
international
HIGHER EDUCATION

RED GLOBE
PRESS

First edition 2013
This edition first published 2018 by
RED GLOBE PRESS

Red Globe Press in the UK is an imprint of Springer Nature Limited,
registered in England, company number 785998, of 4 Crinan Street,
London, N1 9XW.

Red Globe Press® is a registered trademark in the United States,
the United Kingdom, Europe and other countries.

ISBN 978–1–352–00320–8 paperback

This book is printed on paper suitable for recycling and made from fully
managed and sustained forest sources. Logging, pulping and manufacturing
processes are expected to conform to the environmental regulations of the
country of origin.

A catalogue record for this book is available from the British Library.

A catalog record for this book is available from the Library of Congress.

Contents

Acknowledgements

Many people have contributed to this guide and I would like to thank them all. First, my thanks to the students who have discussed their dissertations with me over the years. Without the 'works in progress' and outlines of completed studies this book would not be what it is: a special thank you to the students from Brookes and elsewhere whose work appears here.

Thanks to colleagues at Oxford Brookes University, UK and elsewhere who so generously contributed thoughts for the first edition, from inception to critical review. Thanks also to reviewers who offered generous feedback and advice for this new edition and to Jane Penty (University of the Arts) and Clare Parfitt (University of Chichester) for their advice on new content.

Finally, thanks to Sallie Godwin for her inventive and astute illustrations, and to Helen Caunce, Suzannah Burywood and colleagues in the editing and production teams at Red Globe Press who have been endlessly supportive and creative in making this book happen.

Introduction

This book is designed as a guide for students undertaking an extended piece of research at the end of their undergraduate course of study, or as an introduction to independent research for Masters students.

These projects are described in different ways in different institutions, subject disciplines and countries around the world.

What's in a name?

- **dissertation**
- *research project*
- *thesis*
- *extended essay*
- *research paper*

They all require independent research
at the end of a taught programme of study.

In this book, this independent research is most frequently referred to as a *dissertation* (a UK term) or *research project*. Whatever the language, the prospect of setting out on independent research after a taught programme of study can feel like a step into the unknown:

How can I possibly write 10,000 words?

This is my opportunity to research something I really want to do …

I can't imagine working on my own …

It counts for two credits, so if it's really good I could get a first

This book is designed as a guide on your research journey. It focuses on looking ahead at each stage so that, by anticipating what comes next, you are better prepared for it.

About this book

Planning Your Dissertation is organised in the order in which you carry out each stage of the work for your dissertation or research project. This is shown as *The journey of your dissertation* on pp. xii–xiii. This, as you will see, is quite different to the order in which you finally present the story of your research in the completed project you hand in.

Part 1 Getting started is about the first steps in planning your research paper or dissertation and introduces some key themes that recur through the book.

Part 2 Planning your research ends with an outline of a research plan, and considers the research and project planning that goes into it.

Part 3 Planning your literature review is about the thinking, searching, reading, (thinking more) and planning that goes into a literature review.

Part 4 Thinking about methodology is about the *how* of research: the thinking and planning you need to do to get the outcomes you are looking for.

Part 5 What's in a dissertation? At the heart of the book, this mini dissertation library outlines the structure and content of 12 dissertations. It gives a flavour of the range of formats and structures of dissertations across the disciplines.

Part 6 Writing and argument takes a look at the structures, style and language for writing persuasively.

Part 7 Planning your endgame is about how to showcase your work: how to write a conclusion and introduction and turn your script into a polished finished product.

The journey of your dissertation

TIMELINE

START

PART
1
GETTING STARTED

EXPLORING IDEAS

STRATEGIC PLANNING

SUPERVISOR

READING

RESEARCH QUESTION

TIME PLANNING

PLAN

RESEARCH PLAN

2
PLANNING YOUR RESEARCH

SUPERVISOR

THINK

FINDING IT

AHA!

MAKING SENSE

READING

3
PLANNING YOUR LITERATURE REVIEW

PLANNING

AIM & OBJECTIVES

METHODS TO MATCH

USING THEORY

REFLECT

4
THINKING ABOUT METHODOLOGY

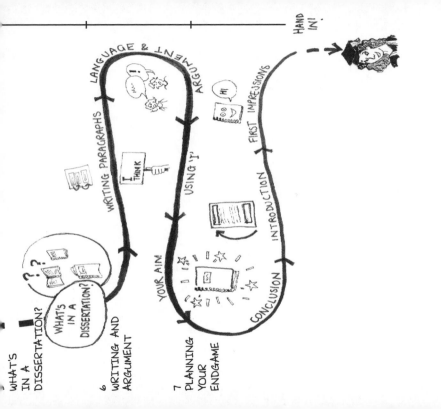

GETTING STARTED

Part 1 outlines the first phase of your journey.

▶ Chapter 1 invites you to stand back and take a strategic overview of what is involved and why you are doing it.
▶ Chapter 2 takes the first step in becoming a researcher – finding an idea that excites you.
▶ You are not alone on this journey. You will have a supervisor to advise you. Chapter 3 is about clarifying this relationship so you can make best use of this guidance.

That said, you are embarking on an independent study, and you are both the **researcher** and the **project manager** of this project.

Why do a dissertation?

The end-of-course dissertation enables you to show that you can do the sort of research you have been learning about throughout your course of study. It will also demonstrate your personal and project management skills: your ability to

▶ work independently
▶ develop a mature and effective working relationship with your supervisor
▶ manage the project from start to finish – making practical arrangements and meeting deadlines
▶ make an in-depth study of a topic relevant to your future career plans.

Ask strategic questions

The six strategic questions[1] are really helpful in project planning and the answers will help to bring your dissertation into sharp focus.

---

1 Used in other books in this series: *Getting critical* pp1–6, *Time management* pp39–44, *Reflective writing* pp16–20.

Read your course materials carefully, and check and recheck regularly online to make sure you have all the information available.

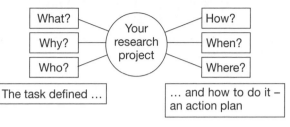

What exactly do you have to DO? The task defined

Try asking yourself the first three strategic questions, using the prompts below.

What exactly are you being asked to produce?	
How is it described? *Research project? Dissertation? Practical dissertation? Thesis? Research paper? Other?*	
How long/number of words? Are references and the 'preliminary pages' (title page, acknowledgements, abstract, contents etc.) included in the word count or not?	
What is the guidance about structure, chapters? How many? What goes in them? Approx. length of each?	
Are you given guidance about presentation? Eg font/size, margins, headings, cover sheets?	

Why are you doing a dissertation?	
External reasons: required for an Honours degree, attractive to an employer …	
Internal reasons: a question you want to answer, a need you have identified, personal satisfaction, to excel in your studies …	

Who are you writing for?	
Your primary reader will be a colleague of your supervisor: you have time to get to know what they are looking for.	
Other(s)? Eg work placement mentor. They could be the second reader/examiner in a work-related project. What do they want to see in it?	
Who will help you? What is the role of your supervisor? Who else can help? Librarian, lab technician, contacts?	

As you note down your answers to the first three strategic questions, your project will begin to take shape and become more manageable.

Getting it done – an action plan

Take a few more moments to work through the last three strategic questions – checking through the information you have. The ones below will help you clarify the practicalities.

When are your deadlines?	
When is the deadline for the final hand-in of the bound copy? The deadline for electronic submission?	
What are the interim deadlines for each phase/chapter? For registration and other forms to submit? Is there a set schedule or do you have to create your own?	
When are the key meetings and contacts with your supervisor/course team?	

Where will you do your research?	
Your research and reading? Your uni library? Any other?	
If you plan to do primary research, where will that be? What planning do you need to do for access, permissions, ethical approval? Other practicalities – cost, fares, time, room booking etc.?	

How will you do it?	
This is what this book is about! And your supervisor will guide you.	

You may be given a clear outline of the stages of your project in lectures, schedules and helpful notes. Equally, you may find you have surprisingly little detailed guidance. If, after you've worked through your course materials and had a go at answering the six strategic questions, you are still not clear, take control and ask.

Meanwhile, start thinking like a researcher …

2 Exploring ideas

Research starts with an idea, a question, an observation – something you'd like to know more about. This is what makes an independent study different. It is your opportunity to research something that interests YOU.

An idea may pop up from anywhere

It could be triggered by …

a news item   an incident at work

a previous course

an experience you've had yourself … or involving family or a friend

a personal interest

something you've read … or observed

something useful to your future career

You may already have an idea for your dissertation. Explore it a bit. First, widen it out – see all the directions it could go in.

Workshop 1: A brainstorm

→ Take a large sheet of paper – A3 is ideal.

→ In the centre draw a circle. In it write your topic with only as much detail as you are confident about right now. If that is quite general, put that down. If you are quite specific in your focus, write that.

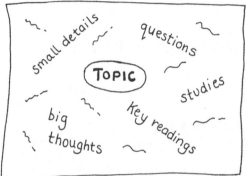

→ Fill the rest of the sheet with everything that pours out of your mind in any order ... anything and everything. Don't worry about connecting them – that can follow.

→ Just go for it – take five minutes.

My placement asked me to study one of their services. Something around parents and play.

My dad wasn't allowed to use his medication for diabetes when he went into hospital. Why not?

I'd like to work for a company that takes 'corporate social responsibility' seriously. Are there any?

I'm a yoga teacher and I know it helps people with back pain. I'd like to find out the scientific evidence ...

It would be good if a new machine for testing samples could be shown to be as reliable as the current slower system ...

I've always loved the outdoors but what opportunities for outdoor play do children get today?

I'd like to work as a wind engineer – I'm doing my dissertation on this.

I come from Greece and study History in the UK. I noticed that Greece features very little on modern European history syllabi, despite the important role it often played.

I'm interested in the links between fitness, heart rate and common health conditions.

I'm puzzled by five Year 3 children who just can't write. Why is this?

I hadn't realised how massive HIV/AIDS is till I went to South Africa. There must be other ways of combating it ...

I'm studying tourism but my country is in conflict. What future is there for the tourist industry?

I became genuinely interested in changing lifestyles and the sociology of food and dining out ...

As a student nurse I noticed that many of the residents react very positively to music ...

All these ideas are meaningful. They touch on issues that matter in the real world – a problem to investigate, a question to answer. They emerge at the point where personal interest or experience meets a topic area the student touched on in their course.

Can you add your idea here?

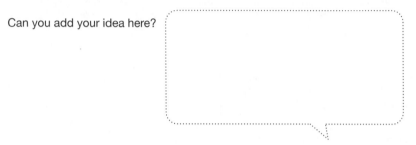

Initial ideas grow and change. Part 5 shows outlines of many of the completed dissertations that started with ideas here.

Still stuck?

If your ideas need a bit of coaxing, think methodically about topics and courses you have studied previously.

Workshop 2: Searching for a topic

- → Take a large sheet of paper – A3 is ideal.
- → In the centre draw a circle. In it write 'I'd like to find out more about ...'
- → Draw more circles around the big circle, each containing one course or topic area you have previously studied.
- → Take your time ...

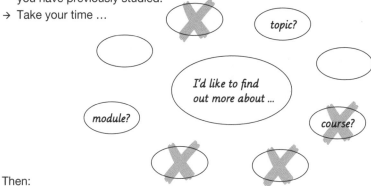

Then:
- → Cross out any you are not particularly interested in.
- → Look at the ones left. Explore these some more.

Where have you got to?

Test out your topic one more time:

▶ Does it interest you?

▶ Does it matter?

Why?
Why?

If you can explain *why*, you have two key qualities of a researcher:

▶ If it interests you, you will be more able to do the detective work in finding out more about it. Your interest will help you keep motivated in the months ahead …

▶ If what you are researching matters (to you, to your workplace, to others), you will be able to articulate why you are researching it. You have a *rationale* for your research.

The first sessions are likely to be lectures or group sessions. Do attend these – they lay the ground for your first meeting with your supervisor. Time is precious, and face-to-face time is particularly precious as it is limited. Make good use of it.

Who advises you?
▶ *Supervisor*
▶ *Teaching assistant*
▶ *Lecturer*
▶ *Adviser*
▶ *Assistant professor*
▶ *Faculty*
▶ *Staff*
▶ *Course team*

Key advisers may have any of these roles.

Meeting your supervisor

Bring to the meeting:

▶ your ideas for what you want to research
▶ any questions or clarifications you want to ask.

Take from the meeting:

▶ your supervisor's feedback on your research topic/question
▶ clarity on how you will work with your supervisor
▶ guidance on your next steps.

Supervisors work in different ways, and while some of the answers to the questions below may be in the guidance, it is a good idea to check them with your supervisor.

Ground rules checklist	Notes
What is the total number of hours your supervisor has to supervise you?	
What does this time allocation include? 1:1, group tutorials, whole group sessions, email, reading drafts?	
Does your supervisor have a suggested schedule of meetings/contacts and deadlines?	

Ground rules checklist	Notes
How do you contact your supervisor? By email? In what circumstances (if any) is mobile contact acceptable?	
How often are meetings?	
What if you can't make a meeting? Or need to change one? What notice do you give?	
What preparation does s/he want you to do before each meeting?	
How will you keep a record of meetings? Notes? Record it? Email a record of key points?	
What kind of feedback will your supervisor give you (written, verbal)? At what points?	
When is your supervisor available and not? Note holiday periods when s/he is away for some time.	
What should you do next?	

Part 1 has outlined the first steps in your dissertation journey.

**1
GETTING STARTED**

With an idea to take you forward, and a clear idea of the practicalities involved, you can move on with both your research and the project planning.

Once your supervisor has approved your idea, you can get going on your research.

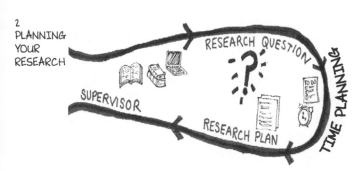

A research plan (or 'proposal') is a useful milestone and may also be a course requirement. Part 2 is about the thinking, reading and planning that underpins your research plan:

▶ starting the reading to check your idea is researchable and to find your focus or 'angle' (Chapter 4)
▶ developing your initial idea into a working research question (Chapter 5)
▶ time planning for a longer project (Chapter 6).

A practical point

If you plan to carry out any primary research, start making arrangements as soon as possible. Check:

▶ **access** to the setting (people, organisations, locations, equipment)
▶ **processes** such as ethical approval, permissions, requests.

It all takes longer than you think.

Read to find out about your topic area – to check that your idea is researchable, to discover what is known out there, to find your focus or 'angle' in a big field. This 'background' or 'preliminary' reading will lay the foundations for your literature review.

The 'literature' is a broad term to cover 'any printed matter' – and of course electronic sources – on which you can draw in your research. Books and chapters are a useful introduction and journal articles are the best source for current research. You may also need to refer to statistics, reports (government, company) and the great wealth of information you can find on the web.

Literature:
The body of works that treat of a subject (1860). Any printed matter (1895). Shorter Oxford Dictionary

Consider things like:

▶ Do you have enough *baseline knowledge* to make sense of what's out there? If you choose something you are familiar with, you are better able to judge the relevance of material you find.

▶ What *themes* or *topics* do you see in the discussions? Choose a topic that relates to issues in your programme of study.

- What *concepts* or *theories* are current in your topic area? You will be expected to use these to frame your research.
- What are the *debates*? You will be expected to show you are familiar with different explanations, perspectives, policies or practices.
- What *studies* have other people done in related areas? How did they do them?

What kind of sources are you looking for?

This (of course) depends on your subject and question. Take a look at past reading lists: websites, books, chapters, journal articles both academic and professional. What *type* of literature are they? This is a good indication of the type of literature you should be looking for in your research. Think about:

Four types of literature		
1	Theoretical	Presents models and theories for interpreting and explaining patterns in practice.
2	Research	Describes systematic enquiries into policy and practice.
3	Practice	Written by informed professionals who evaluate each other's practice and by practitioners who evaluate their own practice.
4	Policy	Proposes changes in practice that are desired by policy makers.

Source: Wallace and Wray (2011, p95).

Turn your idea into a question … and see how you can link the elements of your question to 'the literature'.

These examples show this next step for three of the ideas on p9.

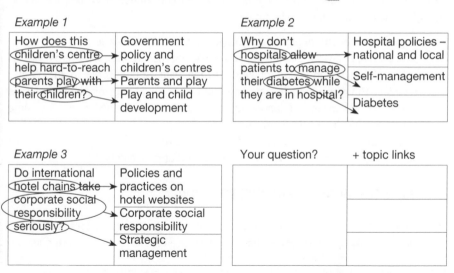

Example 1

How does this children's centre help hard-to-reach parents play with their children?	Government policy and children's centres
	Parents and play
	Play and child development

Example 2

Why don't hospitals allow patients to manage their diabetes while they are in hospital?	Hospital policies – national and local
	Self-management
	Diabetes

Example 3

Do international hotel chains take corporate social responsibility seriously?	Policies and practices on hotel websites
	Corporate social responsibility
	Strategic management

Your question?	+ topic links

Does this initial reading give you confidence that your question is worthwhile? That it touches on themes rooted in your area of study? That the material is out there and you can find it?

If the answer is 'no', don't give up. It could be that your question is not yet focused enough to be researchable. It might be:

▶ Too topical, too recent for high-quality research to be published yet.
  For example, as I write this (2018), you could not research the long-term political impact of the collaboration of North Korea with South Korea in the Winter Olympics. But you could research the long-term impact of previous Olympics on internal and external relations of other host countries, and draw out some possibilities for Korea's future relationships.
▶ Too vague, broad and unknowable in its present form.
  You need to work on it, to make it more focused and researchable.

Making it researchable: finding your angle

Ciara wants to develop a personalised intervention for five Year 3 children (age 7–8) who are not making progress in writing, and to research this for her dissertation.

First, she wants a better understanding of the problem. She looks to the literature:

Why are these five children not making progress with writing?	Child development
	Theories on emergent writers
	Government policies and reviews, National Curriculum

Source: Ciara Fagan (student, Education) with thanks.

But this is all about younger children – nothing to help with my problem of the 7/8 year olds who aren't making progress with writing.

This is more than a gap. It's a void!! Help! I'll have to change my topic …

No, don't change your topic! This is a great topic. It matters, it's meaningful; your findings will make a difference. Stay with it.

Time for reflection … Am I missing something?

In each case, their English is fluent but, on reflection, not their first language … Can they write in their first language? Does this matter?

Might it have something to do with cognition?

And more possible avenues for inquiry open up. Research sometimes goes in a straight line, one step after another. More often, you find you have more thinking to do. Just when you think you have nailed it, your research question slips away, and you go back to asking more questions. But it will be the better and richer for it.

Workshop 3: Thinking around your question

When you have done some reading, go back to your original question and try mapping the questions you can now see. You are looking for avenues to go down, possible explanations, lines of inquiry.

→ Take a sheet of paper.
→ Put your topic, problem or question at the bottom.
→ Ask *three* questions, drawing both on your original thoughts and on new perspectives from your reading.
→ For each, add possible answers, thoughts, further questions.
→ Reflect on the ones you want to follow up.

You are looking for a line of inquiry that really interests or intrigues you – an issue you want to know more about. Start searching, and as you read you may start to see themes and debates about your issue in 'the literature'.

As more questions follow you will also begin to see the 'story' your research could tell – and the focus for your literature review.

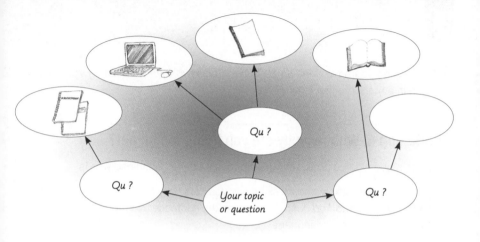

Your literature review should be a story with a beginning, a middle and an end. It is a synthesis that links ideas or finds differences. It is not a list. (Thomas 2017, p63)

Try rerunning Workshop 3 again, refocusing each time on a new line of inquiry, till you have something you are happy to take forward.

All the thinking you have done so far is the groundwork for articulating your research question in a more precise form.

> **Workshop 4: <u>What exactly</u> are you <u>trying</u> to <u>find out</u>?**
>
> Read this question out loud with the emphasis on the underlined words.
>
> Now answer it as simply and as clearly as you can.
> → Start: *'I'm trying to find out …'* and finish the sentence. No more.
> → Write it down in plain language.
>
> | I'm trying to find out … |
> | .... |
> | .... |

You may just have written down your research question. Test it out.

▶ Is it clear to you?
▶ Is it short? A single sentence?
▶ Is it specific? Does it have a single focus?
▶ Does it point you to two or three different areas of literature?

Reconsider your question if:

▶ it has lots of bits to it. Some of these may be sub-questions which you can include as objectives (see p69), but take them out of your main research question
▶ it is too broad or general. A more specific question will enable you to achieve more depth
▶ you are not happy with it. You are the best judge of whether your question matches what you really want to know.

I'm trying to find out …

The students above (p21) now have a working question to drive their research:

▶ How does a children's centre support hard-to-reach parents in playing with their children?

▶ What prevents patients from managing their diabetes while in hospital?

▶ How do international hotel chains implement Corporate Social Responsibility in their business plans?

The exact wording may change, but the focus is clear.

Do you now have a working question?

Do you now have a working question to drive your research? Write it down.

Time planning a longer project

A longer project has distinct phases: a beginning, a middle, and an end – your deadline. On the one hand, you need to maintain an overview of the whole journey to see what lies ahead and to keep on schedule. On the other, you need to make sure you don't try to micro-plan into the far distant future. You want to see the whole and plan the detail as it comes into focus.

Three stages for planning a longer project

1 **The bigger picture**: deadlines through to hand-in.
2 **The next milestone**: completing a phase/chapter/section/meeting with your supervisor.
3 **The week ahead**: your TO DO list.

Time planning 1: the bigger picture[2]

Plan this quite loosely: the whole journey, and the milestones and deadlines on the way.

---

2 *Time management* in this series takes a closer look at time-planning strategies that may help you with planning and juggling other commitments.

Workshop 5: The way ahead

Try to visualise your pathway from where you are now (don't look back and include what you've done up to now) to when you hand in your completed dissertation/project.

→ Take a large sheet of paper – A3 is ideal.
→ Put yourself at the bottom: **start**.
→ Show your completion point and date at the top: **finish**.
→ Sketch the journey in between.
→ Mark in the phases of the task.
→ Show the trouble spots and milestones – bits you think you will find tricky, bits you will find stimulating, or straightforward.
→ Mark in the deadlines on the way – set by your supervisor or yourself.

Give yourself 10 minutes.

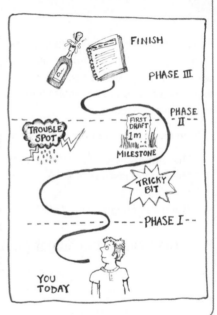

Be realistic! You have other important commitments – other assignments, family, job, sport – a social life, even. Your timeline needs to take these into account.

Now you can plan the phases of your research. What has to be completed before the next phase can start? What do you have to start before your current phase is finished?

Time planning 2: the next milestone

Ideal time plans are … well … ideal! In an ideal world you might have started that bit earlier … but you are where you are. Start from TODAY!

A rough timeline (Workshop 5) may work fine for you. If you are asked to include an *action plan* or *timeline* in a research plan, a Gantt chart gives a neater appearance.

Phase in your research	Month					
	▬					
	▬▬▬▬▬ ▪▪▪▪▪▪▪▪					
	▬▬▬ ▪▪▪▪▪					
	▬▬▬▬▬					
	▬▬▬▬▬					
	▬▬▬▬					

Time planning 3: your TO DO list

You do need to micro-plan the week ahead, and what you want to do in each day. This is the point where you have to juggle all the things to do with your life (job, kids, friends, chores) with the small steps towards your project.

Aim to do something towards your research every day – no matter how small. Put this, along with everything else you have to do, on your TO DO list for

▶ each week
▶ each day.

And tick them off when you've done them.[3]
It's a great feeling!

---

3 See *Time management* in this series (pp2–7) for more on TO DO lists.

Your research plan draws together all the work you have done up to now: your knowledge of the themes of your topic from your reading; the development of your research question. Add to this a plan of action and you will have a useful plan that will help you visualise the phases of the work involved from now to hand-in – and convince your supervisor that you are in control.

There is no set format for a project or research plan. Different institutions, disciplines and departments will vary in the detail of exactly what they require, but there is a common core.

Remember the strategic questions (p3)?

Any research plan needs to offer your reader answers to these key project-planning questions.

Below are points to consider under each question. You may think of others. Check which you will be expected to include and in what order.

Research plan

Your topic	WHAT?
Topic/broad area of interest Working title, research question, or aim Specific objectives or sub-questions	

Rationale
Rationale or 'justification' of your question: why are you doing it? Why does it matter? Is there a gap you want to fill? Your personal motivation

WHY?

Think about WHO will be reading this and what they expect to see

Outline of approach
Reading: Outline of relevant literature You could be asked to present this as a: ▪ short *Context* or *Background* section (referenced) ▪ 'map' of topic areas ▪ list of key sources ▪ annotated bibliography ▪ notes on a small number of key sources

A number of HOW? questions

Research design and approach
Here's how I'm going to do it and justification: why *this* way? Why these theories, frameworks, methods?

Project management
Will you carry out any first-hand or primary work?

Logistics: the setting/organisation; getting access, contacts,
permissions, costs, specialist resources
Documentation: such as ethics and safety forms (if applicable)

Action plan

To show the time you allocate to each phase
of your research, interim and final deadlines

Ask yourself one last uncomfortable
question: *What could go wrong?*

If you can see problematic personal
circumstances, plan to bring *forward*
your deadlines. The unexpected is …
well … unexpected. Build in extra
time.

ERROR!

The supervisor's perspective

For many students, the dissertation or research project marks a transition into the world of work or further study. Some supervisors introduce this external perspective:

▶ *If I was thinking about publishing your project, how would you sell it to me?*
▶ *Time is money. If you multiply the number of hours you spend on your dissertation by the £$ you are paid at work, what do you get? How do you persuade me that your project is worth that?*

This may not be your perspective, and it may not be your supervisor's. Your dissertation will cost you a lot of time and effort and of course you want it to be good: it may also be a shop window for your next step into work or study. Food for thought.

The supervisor perspective

I prefer to think of my role as 'mentor' – more guide than director. It changes the relationship.

Students have been told to make a 30-minute appointment every two weeks. Good students do …

I tell students not to take notes during a supervision and to concentrate on the discussion. Record it – and replay it later.

I expect students to make notes during a supervision, write them up and email them to me afterwards.

If students miss a supervision, it's hard to make it up. The ones who don't attend supervisions or don't submit drafts are the ones who fail.

We expect to see the completed Student Record of Supervision at the last supervision.

The deadlines your supervisor sets are mandatory – non-negotiable.

We set out in writing what students can expect from supervisors and what supervisors expect of students.

Some students just don't get that this is an independent study – they expect me to give them articles to read and no, I don't write it for them!

Some students don't get it that supervisors have a strict allocation of time and this includes reading and giving feedback on drafts. It's not all face to face …

What's missing from these comments is the warmth, enthusiasm and admiration supervisors often feel about their students and their projects:

> It's a real joy to see students doing independent work, to see someone branch out, with their own ideas, their own methods.

(Nick Swarbrick, Lecturer, Education)

By this point your research is well under way: you have a working question; a clear direction for your reading; a better understanding of the role of your supervisor – and a project plan to work to. It is time to move on to the next phase of your research: the literature review.

PLANNING YOUR LITERATURE REVIEW

The literature review is often the first chapter you write. Here you show the knowledge you have gained and the debates you have engaged with. You organise your write-up to lead your reader to your research question and show them the purpose of your research.

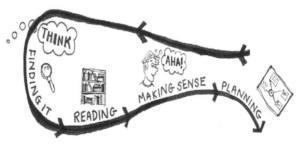

3
PLANNING
YOUR
LITERATURE
REVIEW

FINDING IT · THINK · READING · AHA! · MAKING SENSE · PLANNING

This review of the literature may be in a single chapter (see Dissertations 2, 7, 8, 10) or two chapters (Dissertations 5, 6). It may be part of the introduction (Dissertations 1, 4). Where chapters are thematic (Dissertations 9, 11), it may not be appropriate to use the term 'literature review' at all.

The steps in organising your research and reading for your literature review are to:

▶ think about what you're looking for (Chapter 9)
▶ find it (Chapter 10)
▶ read it (Chapter 11)
▶ make sense of it (analyse and synthesise) (Chapter 12)
▶ and then plan the structure of this section (Chapter 13).

Part 3 outlines these steps. Writing is considered in Part 6.

In going back to the themes you identified in your initial reading, you are in a different place to where you were then. You now know that this is a worthwhile, researchable issue, and you have the tools to get going:

▶ **a working question** to point you to two or three directly related topic areas
▶ **a purpose:** to find the specific strands that will help you answer your research question.

You want to find out …

What is known about your topic areas?	Core knowledge, emerging knowledge, trends
What different approaches and perspectives have other researchers taken?	Concepts, theories and models; studies and case studies
How did they do it?	Could you use or adapt their methods, approach or working tools?

All the time you are asking: how could this help *me* to answer my question?

Primary or secondary sources?

A *primary source* is information collected and written up by the organisation or person who carried out the work at first hand: data collection, a case study, observations, theory, analysis – often published in journal articles.

Secondary sources are written by someone who has read the primary source(s) and summarised or described it in some way – often in a textbook.

Use primary sources wherever you can, and be careful about relying too heavily on secondary sources.

A textbook that summarises a lot of work in the field is a good place to start for an overview. However, you then need to go and find the actual sources so your understanding of the issue is not limited to the short summary in the textbook. You want to get as close as you can to the first-hand experience of the original researcher and use primary sources wherever possible: documents and artefacts, online content, reports, statistics.

See also *Referencing and understanding plagiarism* (2017), pp102–4, in this series.

In reality, your question will point you to the sources you need, whether it's primary, secondary or somewhere in between. The real question to ask is: *What sources will help me to answer my question?*

For example

If your question is to find out ...	you might decide to look at
how people's sexual behaviour changed in [response to particular initiatives to combat] the HIV/AIDS epidemic in Uganda (Tom Georgiou, student, Medicine)	▶ specific studies (in peer-reviewed journals) ▶ raw data (held by the Uganda Ministry of Health and international organisations) ▶ systematic reviews (see p80)
whether Corporate Social Responsibility (CSR) is really taken seriously in international hotel chains (Alice Ogle, student, Business and Hospitality, Dissertation 6)	▶ specific studies (in peer-reviewed journal articles) ▶ online company reports and documentation ▶ trade and special interest publications and websites ▶ theoretical models (books and journal articles)
All are good and appropriate sources for these inquiries.	

And what about your question?

You want to find out ...	so you might want to look at
	▶ ? ▶ ? ▶ ?

About 'quality' in sources

If you haven't actually carried out the research yourself, how do you know it's any good? You have two safeguards:

▶ Look for research that has been tested and validated by experts in the field (published in peer-reviewed journals), or research reports produced by reputable bodies such as government, research institutes, international bodies.

▶ Develop your own critical skills to evaluate anything you think of using. You can try using the six strategic questions (p3)*.

You're always asking yourself

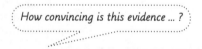

How convincing is this evidence ... ?

Bringing this critical approach to all your reading will help you bring it to your writing.

---

* See *Getting critical* Ch. 6 and *Reading and making notes* Ch. 14 in this series.

Shelf surfing and Google may have served you well enough in the past. Now, however, you need to develop your research and search skills so that you can use databases effectively to target the quality sources you need.

Searching databases

Computers can't think for you, but they are very good at finding, from a database of zillions of articles, ones that include the keywords you ask them to look for. So think carefully, imaginatively and critically. You are looking for the relatively small number of articles where the keywords come together.

> *Example*
> Research question: *How does political instability impact on tourism planning and development? The case of Zedland.*

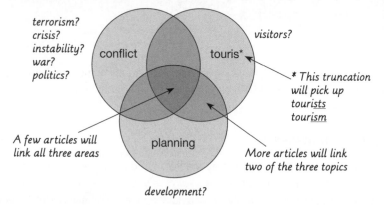

terrorism?
crisis?
instability?
war?
politics?

conflict

visitors?

touris*

* This truncation
will pick up
tour*ists*
tour*ism*

A few articles will
link all three areas

planning

More articles will link
two of the three topics

development?

When you go into the database, you'll see something like this (although you may have to select 'Advanced Search' to get multiple boxes):

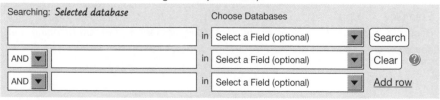

What will you put in the boxes? Try these strategies.

A search strategy in brief

Step	
1	Write down your research question.
2	Choose your keywords – the main ideas.
3	Think of alternative words for the words you circled.
4	Try truncation (touris*) or wildcard (?) in the middle of the word for alternative spellings.
5	Use AND/OR to combine keywords ('Boolean operators'). OR makes your search broader; AND makes it narrower.
6	*5742 results?* To limit your results think about: – publication date/year – language – defining your focus or client group more specifically.
7	List the databases you want to use.

Thanks to Hazel Rothera, subject librarian at Oxford Brookes University, for her kind permission to use this material (adapted) and for her advice that underpins this section.

As you change and focus your search terms, different articles will come up. Yes, you may feel you are going round and round, but you will be getting closer to what you are looking for.

You get what you ask for!

Without changing your search terms at all, you will get very different results depending on the matching you request: whether you are looking for articles with your keyword(s) somewhere in the *full text*, in the *abstract* or in the *title* itself:

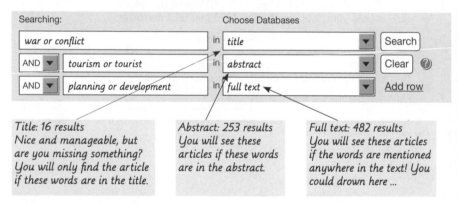

Searching: Choose Databases

war or conflict   in   *title*   Search

AND ▼   *tourism or tourist*   in   *abstract*   Clear ❓

AND ▼   *planning or development*   in   *full text* ▼   Add row

Title: 16 results
Nice and manageable, but are you missing something? You will only find the article if these words are in the title.

Abstract: 253 results
You will see these articles if these words are in the abstract.

Full text: 482 results
You will see these articles if the words are mentioned anywhere in the text! You could drown here ...

Scan your results

A quick search of abstracts produced some likely-looking results. Titles included:

▶ *Deterrents to tourism in Iran*
▶ *The influence of terrorism on international tourism activities*
▶ *From hostile boundaries to tourist attractions*.

Nothing on Zedland, but worth reading the abstracts. Other hits are way off-beam:

▶ *The myth of wild elephants: a social constructive analysis of elephant–human conflicts …*
▶ *The battlefield of the mountain: exploring the conflict of tourism development on the Three Peaks …*

You just have to get in there, trying different combinations logically and thinking creatively, till you find the articles that look as if they will help you answer your question.

> *I can't possibly read all that!*

No, of course you can't read it all – and you don't need to. Think of yourself as a hook, looking for relevant material to fish out …

Read strategically

The shortest and most useful bit of an article is the **abstract** (100–250 words).

- Have a clear sense of what you are looking for: will this help me answer my research question?
- Get familiar with how abstracts are structured in your discipline.
- Use the abstract to help you decide if you want to read more of the article – or move on to the next.

How to read an abstract

Use the strategic questions as a checklist to help you decide if it's worth reading the full text.

What exactly is it about? What did they find out?

Why was the research carried out? What question does it address? The aim?

How did they do it? Why did they do it this way?

An abstract will usually summarise (in a sentence or two):

1 **Aim** or **research question**: why the research was needed
2 **How** they did it
3 **What** they found/the analysis
4 **Conclusions**: the takeaway points.

Who are the researchers? What are their credentials?

When was it published? And carried out? (often some years earlier)

Where was this research carried out? Where is it published? Is the journal peer reviewed?

And then the big one:
So what?
How might it be useful to me?

Will I read the full article? On the basis of this abstract DECIDE:
Do I want to read on?
No? No problem! Next ...!
Yes? Look at the Introduction of the full text

How to read an article

If you decide you want to check out an article, you are not obliged to read it all! Read what you need. You can always go back if you need to.

Contents

Abstract

Chapter 1: Introduction

Chapter 2: Literature review

Chapter 3: Methodology

Chapter 4: Findings

Chapter 5: Discussion

Chapter 6: Conclusions and Recommendations

References

Appendices

The intro will show you:
- *the connection between the research and the bigger issues*
- *the writer's argument for the importance of their research*
- *possibly the theoretical approach taken.*

Are you persuaded that it's relevant to you?
No? Then stop.
Yes? What else will you read?

In science, looking at the figures may tell you the main story, and reduce your reading load.

Still curious or undecided?
Read the conclusions (takeaway points) and/or recommendations or implications – the writer's answer to the So what? question.
Decision! Will you read the rest? If you plan to use it, you do need to read it!

Handy tips and pointers!
Even if you don't read it all, glance at these for useful references, or working tools in the Appendices.

This is an efficient way of reading and well worth trying, especially if you consider yourself to be a slow reader. Going in and out of the article several times should speed up your reading. Your understanding gets better as you become more familiar with the topic or line of reasoning – and of course it is your understanding (not your eye movements) that determines the speed at which you read.

Make notes

To help to secure this understanding, **make notes on what you read**: don't rely on your memory. Include:

- the full reference
- brief summary: main points
- evaluation: strengths and limitations
- reflection: how you might use it.

There are other reasons for writing notes as you go. The act of writing helps you to know what you think. Make sure you record the author (full reference) and what they say *separately* to your thoughts and comments. Like this you will be able to see who said what in your sources, and be able to reference them. Your reader will also be able to hear your distinct 'voice' as author in your writing, and see how you have used and reflected on the material you have read.

For more on critical reading and thinking see other guides in this series: *Getting critical* Part 2; *Reading and making notes; Referencing and understanding plagiarism.*

Analysis

Analysis is the foundation of critical thinking. This is hard thinking, where you disentangle the strands of thoughts and ideas from your new reading and rearrange them in your own way to make sense of them.

This is a crucial step in being able to use the material you read. If you don't STOP and take stock, you may simply end up describing what this study said, what those researchers did, leaving it to your reader to make the connections with what you're doing. They won't: instead they may say …

Your account is rather descriptive. You need to be more analytical.

Your reader will want to see what you are **doing** with your reading. The ability to analyse will lead you on to other critical thinking skills …

The stairway to critical thinking

						Justify
Use critical thinking to develop arguments, draw conclusions, make inferences and identify implications.						Justify
Transfer the understanding you have gained from your critical evaluation and use in response to questions, assignments and projects.					Apply	
Assess the worth of an idea in terms of its relevance to your needs, the evidence on which it is based and how it relates to other pertinent ideas.				Evaluate		
Bring together different sources to serve an argument or idea you are constructing. Make logical connections between the different sources that help you shape and support your ideas.			Synthesise			
		Compare	Explore the similarities and differences between the ideas you are reading about.			
	Analyse	Examine how these key components fit together and relate to each other.				
Start here ☺	Understand	Comprehend the key points, assumptions, arguments and evidence presented.				
Process	Take in the information, i.e. what you have read, heard, seen or done.					

Source: Open University (2008)

Take a look at *Getting critical* (2014) Ch. 14. The sketches and explanations here will help you see what these terms mean in practice.

Synthesis

Synthesis is when you begin to make sense of the themes that emerge from your reading. The groundwork for this is to arrange your sources and reading into two, three or four main themes.

Workshop 6: Mapping your reading

→ Take a sheet of paper – A3 is ideal.
→ Put your question (as it is now) in the middle.
→ Draw a line out for each of the main themes you have identified (two or three?).
→ Use coloured stickies with key points from your reading and stick them near the relevant line.

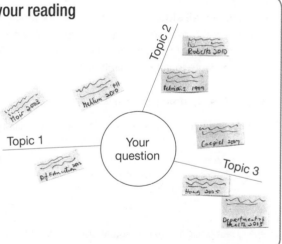

You are now well into your literature review. It's time to draw up a plan for writing. See the examples below and Part 5 for decisions students made.

- **Plan the overall structure**: major themes or topics.
- **Plan the topic areas/sub-themes**: work out the order of your topic areas to see the progression of your argument – the flow that will take your reader from the first words you write to your research question.

Example 1: A children's centre *(Dissertation 7)*

Amina started her lit review with several initial questions:

> Why is play so important for young children?
> Why is play difficult for some parents?
> What can be done to help?

These questions gave her a logical place to start her lit review:

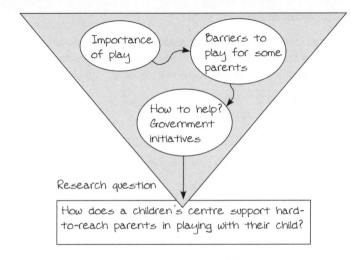

The initial questions firmed up into worthwhile areas to research, drawing in theoretical perspectives as well as policy and practice. This led to the focus and wording of the student's research question.

Amina is now ready to find out for herself what happens in practice and work out the methodology for her primary research.

Example 2: Chronic back pain and yoga

Michaela was interested in the potential of yoga to treat chronic lower back pain (CLBP) and was clear from the start that she wanted to examine the evidence base for this method. In her 'preliminary' literature review she explored both strands of her interest:

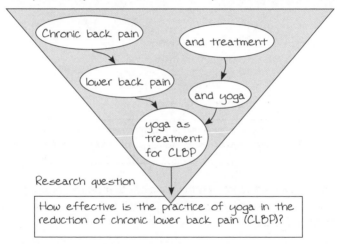

The methodology for this research was the systematic review approach (see Chapter 17 and Dissertation 4).

Example 3: Corporate social responsibility (CSR) *(Dissertation 6)*

Alice started from a single working question – which proved to have several strands and two phases (explored in two chapters). See how they link.

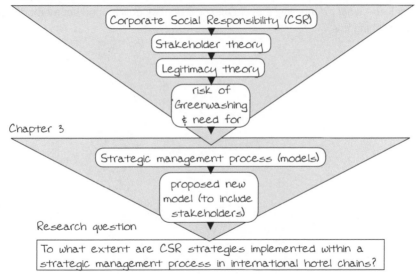

Chapter 2

Corporate Social Responsibility (CSR)

Stakeholder theory

Legitimacy theory

risk of Greenwashing & need for

Chapter 3

Strategic management process (models)

proposed new model (to include stakeholders)

Research question

To what extent are CSR strategies implemented within a strategic management process in international hotel chains?

By linking theories about 'legitimacy' to stakeholder theory, Alice has developed a framework for examining how CSR policies can be implemented through strategic management.

This lays the ground for her examination of the primary evidence of the hotel chains themselves – *what do they say they do* and *how do they do it?* – and her methodology for establishing this.

Example 4: Neoliberalism and inequality *(Dissertation 10)*

Gaia started from a concern about the increasing inequality in India. She wanted to explore the links between this and the economic effects of neoliberalism.

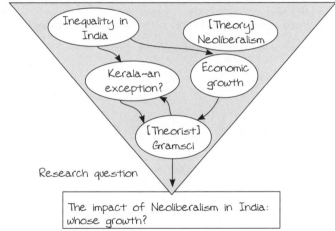

By linking two theoretical analyses, Gaia argues the link between neoliberalism and inequality across India: first, the role of neoliberalism in widening inequality in different aspects of life in India; and second, the theories of Gramsci, in the analysis of an individual state (Kerala).

Workshop 7: Your triangle plan

→ Take a sheet of paper.
→ Draw a large triangle.
→ Map in your areas from broad ... to your aim or research question!

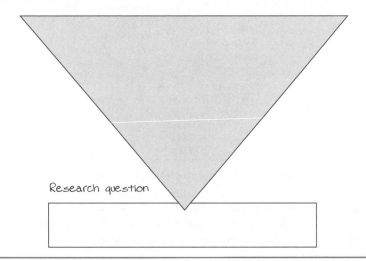

Research question

In your literature review you have shown your reader that you have read, analysed and reflected on the knowledge, interpretations and debates relevant to your research question. You have shown that you are not reinventing the wheel, but 'standing on the shoulders of giants'.

You have made the case for your own research. The answer to your question is not out there in a readily accessible form: there is a gap. You will be providing this answer. The next step is to consider how you will do this.

Back it up! Email it to someone — or yourself!

PART 4
THINKING ABOUT METHODOLOGY

When you have completed your literature review, you are
ready to plan the 'doing' phase of your research.

4
THINKING ABOUT
METHODOLOGY

PLANNING

METHODS TO MATCH

AIM & OBJECTIVES

USING THEORY

REFLECT

What you actually do in your research will depend on your subject discipline, on what you are trying to find out, and, crucially, the decisions you make about how you will go about finding it out – your methodology. Part 4 outlines some of the thinking you need to do before you set off.

You may decide you want to …	See Dissertation
Investigate something yourself and carry out primary research	
– An experiment	1, 2
– Survey and interviews	5
– Observations	7
– Focus groups, interviews	8
– Examination/analysis of products, photos, manuscripts, artefacts	3, 11
Draw together existing theories, models and perspectives in new ways	
– A critique of theories and their impact	9, 10
– Reviewing and adapting models and theory	6
Create a performance, recording or tangible object	
– AND show the underpinning theories and approaches	12
Find the best possible evidence for an intervention or treatment in healthcare	
– By using the 'systematic review' approach	4 and Chapter 17

What a wonderful world of exploration lies behind these headings! You won't be the first person on the planet to explore your area, so there will be approaches to learn and choose from. But you may well be the first person to research that very specific question and that is truly exciting. Methodology is all about HOW you do it …

Your research question has travelled a long way from those initial ideas:

> My placement asked me to study one of their services. Something around parents and play.

> I'd like to find out the scientific evidence ...

> I'd like to work for a company that takes 'corporate social responsibility' seriously.

Your question will now be your guide to *how* you carry out your research. Do check that the question you started out with still accurately reflects exactly what you want to find out. If your focus has shifted in a major or minor way, rewrite it.

Articulating your aim and objectives

You may be required (or choose) to rephrase your question as an AIM and OBJECTIVES. The aim is your overarching purpose, the whole question. The objectives are the sub-questions you need to answer in order to achieve your aim. Your objectives will correspond to the stages of your research – and you can tick them off as you progress.

For example

> **Aim:** To explore and evaluate the extent to which CSR strategies appear to be implemented within the strategic management process of international hotel chains.
>
> **Objectives are to:**
> ☑ review the literature on […], defining and analysing [concepts of x and y]
> ☑ evaluate the literature on [z …]
> ☑ develop a framework that will form the basis of […]
> ☐ analyse and evaluate the application of […] in [*context*]
> ☐ identify limitations and implications for practice and future research
> (Based on Dissertation 6)

Workshop 8: Your aim and objectives

→ Take a sheet of paper.

→ Draw an umbrella.

→ Put your research question *as it is now* in it – your overarching question or aim.

→ Start listing the sub-questions or research areas that contribute to the aim (three to five). These are your 'objectives'.

The ideas students decide to pursue in their research show that the spirit of inquiry is alive and well! When you are clear about exactly what you are trying to find out, your next question is:

What is the best way to do this?

If you concentrate on this you won't be tempted to rush into the first method that comes to mind …

What is expected in your discipline?

Look back to any research methods course or other training you have done (eg lab, work or studio) for guidance on questions like these:

What does your discipline place a high value on?	Yes/no How will you do it?
Showing you understand the research traditions ('paradigms') of your subject?	
Showing you understand different theoretical approaches and their implications?	
Justifying your research approach or design	
Detailing your research methods (so someone else could follow what you did step by step)?	
Showing creativity and its theory base?	
Justifying the kind of data you need to answer your question? What information will you gain from counting or measuring – a *quantitative* method? What will you gain from using *qualitative* methods, such as observation, conversation, interviews, analysis of photographs?	
What specific techniques or **specialist materials** or equipment do you need? Can you access them?	

Why do it that way?

In your methodology you need to show that you have a good reason for doing it this way (and not that way). You need to show:

▶ that you have considered the options for the approaches and specific methods you could use (briefly)

▶ why the approach you took and the specific methods you have chosen will give you the sort of information you need to answer your question, *and*

▶ that you can achieve it from a practical point of view (resources and access), and within your timeframe.

'Theory' is a slippery term: it encompasses the many ways in which the observations of other people are brought together to help to explain and interpret the world around us. It is a sign of being alive and thinking that you can connect your own questions with other people's ways of seeing – the theories, models and frameworks developed by other people who have puzzled over the same problems. You draw on them or adapt them to make sense of what you find.

Theory may be your research …

You may decide to engage directly with theories that try to explain a pattern of behaviour, or a wider trend or phenomenon in society.

▶ In Dissertation 9 Jessica explores sociological theories to explain changes in patterns of eating out.
▶ In Dissertation 10 Gaia points out the widening social inequalities in India and challenges the idea that neoliberalism brings economic benefits to all.

You can use theory to bring new insights to previously researched issues by:

▶ Using a different theory to examine the same issue
▶ Applying well-established theory to a new or different case study, issue or example.

Theory shapes your research ...

In the question you ask

A 'researchable' question points you to the areas of previous research (the 'literature') you need to become familiar with (see Chapter 4).

In identifying a 'gap' in research (for you to fill!)

For example

> *I've always loved the outdoors but I do wonder what opportunities for outdoor play children get today.*

In her lit review this student found a gap in the research – that the 'child's voice' about their experience of outdoor play was largely missing.

To find out about young children's views and attitudes Madelaine studied 10 children. For each, she:

▶ tracked them, noting what each child was doing minute by minute for 20 minutes
▶ had a voice-recorded conversation about activities.

Thanks to Madelaine Chapman for her kind permission to refer to her work.

In how you design your research

Looking at the problem from different perspectives could influence how you carry out your research.

For example
Different theories (or combination of theories/models/frameworks) will bring different perspectives on the issue you want to research.

Different perspectives will lead to different approaches to research.

In the methods you adopt

> *How long does each child play on the climbing frame?*

> *What do children feel about playing on the climbing frame?*

The first question looks nice and easy – it will give you numbers, a **quantitative** outcome. But in practice it could be tricky. What counts as 'on' the climbing frame? Sitting underneath it? Running round it? Then there is the *So what?* question: what does the fact of being on the climbing frame for x minutes tell you about children's views of the experience?

The second question is more obviously tricky: you're looking to elicit accurate responses from young children about 'enjoyment' or 'feelings' – a **qualitative** outcome.

Methods are rarely as simple as they seem! Look to the research methods literature and other studies for ideas and for the debates about the strengths and limitations of the various methods you consider. Make sure you show what you have read (reference it), and say how it has influenced your decisions about how to carry out your research.[4]

---

4 See *Doing research* (2nd edn) in this series (Thomas 2017) for an introduction to research in the social sciences.

In interpreting your findings

The intertwining of theory with practice lies at the heart of developing as a reflective practitioner.

Reflecting on what you do, and on the perspectives of others who have experienced similar things, can offer starting points for analysis. Once you have recorded and organised your findings, you will see themes emerge – another route back to the themes and theories in the subject area your question relates to.

Thanks to Dr Clare Parfitt-Brown, Senior Lecturer in Dance, University of Chichester, for her kind permission to adapt this image from her teaching materials.

And finally … before you meet your supervisor

Do look again at your question (see Workshop 8). If your question has moved or evolved since you last looked at it, make sure your thinking about methodology and the methods you might use has moved with it.

The 'systematic' approach: literature review as methodology

What is a 'systematic' approach?

A review of existing research to answer your specific research question is the methodology now most frequently used in undergraduate and Masters dissertations in healthcare and related subjects.

Students can be confused initially about what this approach involves, especially when it is described as 'literature review as methodology'. Once it can be seen as a methodology in its own right, modelled on the 'systematic review' of evidence for treatments and practices in healthcare, students have a step-by-step path to follow.

Dissertation 4 gives an outline of the 'systematic review' approach and shows what goes where.

What is a 'systematic review'?

How do you know if one treatment will work better than another, or if it will do more harm than good? (Cochrane Collaboration 2013)

'Systematic reviews' in healthcare and health policy were established by The Cochrane Collaboration to provide answers to this crucial question. Cochrane Reviews are internationally recognised as the highest standard in evidence-based healthcare:

> Each systematic review addresses a clearly formulated question; for example:
>
> Can antibiotics help in alleviating the symptoms of a sore throat?
>
> To answer this question, we search for and collate all the existing primary research on a topic that meets certain criteria; we then assess it using stringent guidelines, to establish whether or not there is conclusive evidence about a specific treatment.
> (Cochrane Collaboration 2018)

As a student you are not expected to conduct research to these exacting professional standards! But take a look at the Cochrane website to get a feel for the research tradition of the 'systematic review' approach.

You will, however, be expected to develop a clearly focused question to guide your research.

Why use the systematic approach for your methodology?

You need to articulate the reasons why it is the most appropriate methodology for what you want to find out. Perhaps you:

▶ could not generate the data yourself to answer your question
▶ do not want to limit your inquiry to the routine issues you could uncover through your own primary research
▶ want to develop practices based on the best available evidence
▶ have another reason?

Dissertation 4 gives an outline of the systematic approach and shows what goes where.[5]

The methodology and methods chapter

A 'systematic' approach requires you to be systematic! Keep a notebook or logbook and note down the decisions you make and everything you do at the time (you'll forget very quickly), including things that didn't work out. You will be expected to show each of the steps below in your methodology and methods chapter.

---

5 For detailed advice on literature review as methodology, see Aveyard (2014).

Step 1: How did you develop your research question?

Your decision to research your topic arose from an interest, personal or professional, or both:

> *Why couldn't my dad manage his own diabetes in hospital?*

> *As a student nurse I noticed that many of the residents reacted so positively to music.*

> *I'm a yoga teacher and I just know it helps people with back pain. I'd like to find out the evidence ...*

The studies are out there ... but you will be drawing together studies that have never been viewed together before to answer YOUR question.

To turn your initial interest into an answerable question, you may be expected to structure it by using a particular framework such as PICO. It will help you dissect your question into its component parts and restructure it to make it easier to find answers.

Formulating an answerable question: PICO (and PICOT)

	The framework	*This means being clear about ...*
P	Patient(s)/Population	Profile of patients/subjects you plan to study
I	Intervention/Indicator/ Issue	Treatment/intervention given to the subjects
C	Comparison/Control	A similar group of patients/subjects not having the intervention
O	Outcome	How the effectiveness of the intervention is assessed

PICOT: Time may also be relevant to your study

T	Time	In defining the population, eg by age or the timing of the intervention

Example: Laura's PICO analysis and research question (Dissertation 4)

	The framework	*Laura's PICO analysis*
P	Patient(s)/Population	Adults with diabetes in hospital (for unrelated treatment)
I	Intervention/Indicator	Self-management of diabetes
C	Comparison/Control	Self-management of diabetes not encouraged/permitted
O	Outcome	Barriers to self-management of diabetes identified

Her father's experience in hospital started Laura thinking. Using the PICO framework led Laura to the focus and wording of her research question:

What are the barriers to patients managing their diabetes as in-patients?

Step 2: Develop your search strategy

Follow the process outlined on p47.

Step 3: Work out your inclusion/exclusion criteria and use them

Decide what you really need from the studies to help answer your question. These are your criteria for including – and excluding – studies for your review.

Step 4: Read the abstracts and then the full text of articles on your shortlist

Apply your criteria to each abstract to select articles that meet your criteria for inclusion. Read the full text of those that really look relevant. Exclude those that do not.

Step 5: Other searching: have you missed anything?

Check:

▶ leading journals in the field for the past year
▶ websites of key organisations
▶ full reports where you have found a summary.

In short, use your initiative to find sources that could help you, or satisfy yourself that they are not there.

Step 6: Identify themes

As you read your target articles you will see common themes emerging. Coding papers is a methodical way of doing this – mark each time a particular theme emerges.

Step 7: Decide on your method to critically appraise your papers

In healthcare this is likely to be one or more of the 'tools' in the Critical Appraisal Skills Programme (CASP, no date).

Your supervisor and taught sessions will probably go into more detail on this. Ask if you are unclear.

So, on to your results chapter

Use themes for your analysis: with your chapter organised under themes as headings you will not be tempted to simply retell the 'story' of your articles. You will become analytical as you pull points from several articles to explore the findings on each theme.

For example: Laura (Dissertation 4) identified four themes in her analysis.

1 Hospital systems as a barrier to self-management
2 Staff not handing control of management of diabetes to patients
3 Individual patients' abilities to manage their diabetes
4 Patients' reluctance to manage their diabetes

It's fine to conclude that the evidence is weak: *There is some evidence that ... but ....* It shows your integrity as a researcher and that you can see the complexity of knowledge in these fields.

The key point to take away from Part 4 is the importance of thinking for yourself HOW you will carry out your research. You gain ideas from the studies you read, you look at how others in your field pursued similar inquiries, you read about the different methodologies used in your field. Finally, you make decisions about how you will carry out your research.

This is what makes this central period of the research project such an enjoyable and satisfying one.

Keep in touch with your supervisor!

Stay in touch during this time of DOING and WRITING UP your research by email or face to face. Read any feedback you get carefully and reflect on how to use it.

Enjoy!

> Back it up! I use Dropbox – I can access it anywhere.

Part 5 is different to the other sections. It doesn't *tell* you anything. It is a mini library of 12 dissertations for you to browse and reflect on.

All the students whose dissertations are outlined here received good marks. They all illustrate formats well used in each discipline. None are 'models' to copy, but they will show you what a completed dissertation looks like in a range of subject areas and the different ways they can be structured. This should help you work out for yourself the structure that best suits your inquiry.

The dissertations are organised in broad discipline-related groupings:

Science/technology/healthcare/business/social science/education/humanities/arts/creative

If you have the opportunity to look at past dissertations in your subject area do take it! (Check they are good ones!) Look at:

▶ preliminary pages: title page, official paperwork, abstract, acknowledgements
▶ contents: chapter structure and titles; subheadings and numbering
▶ chapters: what goes where; relative length of each
▶ introduction and conclusion, and the link between them
▶ use of illustrations
▶ appendices and references
▶ evidence of coherence, progression and argument
▶ writing style.

While you are browsing, note the style and wording of the titles. It may help you decide on the final wording of your title. Titles can take various forms:

Title form	Example
Question	*What are the barriers to patients managing their diabetes in hospital?* (Dissertation 4)
Statement	*The political ecology of HIV/AIDS in the Eastern Cape, South Africa* (Dissertation 8)
Catchy bit + statement of what you researched	*Measuring counts? The role of design in maintaining healthy behaviours* (Dissertations 3, 6, 7)
Statement + catchy question	*The impact of neoliberalism in India: whose growth?* (Dissertation 10)

Whatever you decide about the final wording, try and keep your working title as a question. If you're always thinking about a question, it helps you see your research as a journey towards finding answers. This will make you more questioning, more evaluative, and reduce the temptation to just describe your research and reading.

Working with your supervisor

Your supervisor will be a crucial source of advice on organisation and structure. The more detail you can show them early on, the better they will be able to advise you.

Scientific knowledge develops by 'standing on the shoulders of giants' – each researcher takes the next step from what has been established by previous research. A science student (Dissertations 1 and 2) works within this tradition. Research in these disciplines places a high value on each step being crystal clear (especially in the methodology) so the reader can judge reliability, quality of evidence and could replicate the work themselves.

Technology (Dissertation 3) is about applying scientific principles to a practical project to bring about change.

Dissertation 1: Biomedical science

Title:

Evaluation of an automated urine analyser for use as a negative screen on urine samples

Abstract
The current situation: the problem
The investigation: what was done and how
What was found
Conclusion and recommendation
(300 words)

Introduction/Literature review:
the current state of knowledge, from broad to narrow:
1.1 The urinary tract
1.2 Incidence and infection
1.3 Pathogens and pathogenesis
1.4 Treatment
1.5 Laboratory diagnosis
1.6 Aims of the project

Materials and methods
2.1 Materials
2.2 Methods

Results
Presented in numbered subsections in tables and figures with brief explanations

Appendices
The documentation of the research:
    safety (COSHH)
    risk assessment
    detailed results (raw data)

Discussion
4.1 Study population: unintended bias in data group
4.2 The machine tested: strengths and limitations
4.3 Potential of machine – cautiously positive
4.4 Interpretation of results linked to previous findings in the literature
4.5 Future investigation and suggested improvements

Conclusion
Positive indications ... but larger study needed for a more accurate assessment

Thanks to Laura Dunn (student, Biomedical Sciences) and to the John Radcliffe Hospital, Oxford, UK, for their kind permission to include this reference to her work.

Dissertation 2: Sport science

Title: *Relationships between heart rate variability, aerobic fitness and blood glucose concentration in healthy men and women*

Abstract
Context: previous work and aim
What was done (participants and measurements)
Key findings

Introduction
Short five-paragraph intro leading to:
Main aim
Additional objective

Review of the literature
> Effects of exercise on ... (A)
> Effects of exercise on ... (B)
> Effects of (A) on (B)
Summary: potential of the proposed intervention

Contents
Abstract
1 Introduction
2 Review of the literature
3 Methods and subjects
4 Results
5 Discussion
References
Appendices

Methods and subjects
3.1 Subjects
3.2 Experimental design
3.3 Assessment of (x)
3.4 Assessment of (y)
3.5 Assessment of (z)
3.6 Statistical analysis

Results
Heart rate variability recordings (+ subsections)
Evaluation of ...
Measurement of ...
Multiple regression analyses

Discussion
Limitations (number of subjects, experimental design, missing data)
Discussion of results in relation to findings from the literature re:
Main aim
Additional objective
Conclusion
> key findings (consistent with the literature)
> restatement of aims
> usefulness of method and future research

Thanks to Luca Cardilli (student, Sport and Exercise) for his kind permission to refer to his work.

Dissertation 3: Product design

Title: *Measuring counts? The role of design in maintaining healthy behaviours*

Abstract
Brief statement of argument [design can offer alternative strategies to maintain healthy behaviours]

Introduction
Argument for the research:
– the problem [failure of self-monitoring devices to improve health outcomes]
Aim and overview of chapters

Contents
Abstract
1 Introduction
2 Literature review and critique
3 Design strategy and analysis
4 Conclusion
References
List of images

Literature review and critique
Analysis of the problem
2.1 Changing health and healthcare
– What is good health?
– A new model for personal healthcare
2.2 Self-monitoring for self-improvement: the problems
Conclusion: design can shape behaviour change and improve health outcomes

Design strategy and analysis
Six design strategies (derived from theory) are explored in an analysis of six products
3.1–3.6
Design strategy/Design product analysis

Conclusion
– Summary of the argument and evidence
– Application of theory and design analyses [to behaviour change in health]
– Need for future research [in the emerging area of 'Behaviour design']

Thanks to Sherif Maktabi (student, Product Design) for his kind permission to refer to his work.

Dissertation 4: Healthcare

A 'systematic' approach: literature review as methodology.

The 'systematic' approach (or 'literature review as methodology') is the most used form of dissertation in this subject area. The structure of each chapter is quite specific. See also Ch. 17 and Ch. 10 for more on this form of dissertation.

Title: *What are the barriers to patients managing their diabetes as in-patients?*

Abstract:
Aim
Methods
Results
Conclusion

Introduction
Overview of chapter
  Research question or aim
1 Overview of main literature
  Definitions
  – Area 1
  – Area 2
  – Area 3
2 Why this topic?
Personal/professional interest + gap in evidence
Outline of chapters

Contents
Abstract
1 Introduction
2 Methodology and methods
3 Results
4 Discussion
5 Conclusion and recommendations
References
Appendices

Thanks to Laura Warnock (student, Adult Nursing) for her kind permission to refer to her work.

Methodology and methods
Overview of chapter
1 Methodology
- Why you chose the systematic review approach
2 Methods
- How you developed your research question
- Search strategy
- Inclusion and exclusion criteria
- Other methods of searching
- Identify themes
- Critical appraisal tools (CASP)

Closing remarks: summary and what next

Results
Overview of chapter
Summary table: analysis of research studies
Critical appraisal of studies organised by theme:
- Theme 1
- Theme 2
- Theme 3
- Theme 4

Conclusion: what stands out? + link to next

Discussion
Overview of chapter, outlining organisation:
- What is established
- What remains unclear
  [eg how strong/weak is the evidence?]
- Limitations of the methods of studies
- Limitations of my research

Conclusion: to what extent do the studies answer my research question?

Conclusion
Takeaway points about:
- the strength of evidence
- practice implications
- personal learning; what I'd do differently next time

Recommendations (as appropriate) for:
- the practice setting
- future research (focus and methods)

Appendices
Material your reader needs to supplement your text, eg:
- Detailed search processes if not included in text
- Critical appraisal tool(s) (eg CASP)
- Correspondence that influenced your research, eg with workplace mentor on ideas for research

Business/education/social science

'Social science' spans a huge range of human experiences and activity. Formats for dissertations are flexible to encompass the range of these inquiries. Your dissertation may have a structure like one of Dissertations 5–10 or have features of more than one.

Start by locating your topic in the landscape of what is already known – the 'literature'. Then think about HOW you will set about answering your research question.

▶ What will your approach be? What theory/body of knowledge will you draw on?
▶ Can you find the answer by researching existing sources?
▶ Do you need to carry out first-hand primary research as well?

If 'yes' to this:

▶ explain your approach
▶ explain why you need to carry out primary research yourself
▶ justify your choice of methods
▶ show how you did it.

Dissertations 5–8 use various forms of theory to frame primary research. Dissertations 9 and 10 use theory as a way to gain a better understanding of a problem or phenomenon and do not use primary research. Check out that Research Methods course. Now's when you need it!

Dissertation 5: Business

Title: *Redefining 'Revenue Management Culture'*

Abstract
Aim and context
Findings from literature
Findings from primary research
Conclusion and recommendation

Introduction
1.1 Introduction to topic area
1.2 Rationale
1.3 Aim and objectives
1.4 Omissions and assumptions
Chapter structure

Literature review
Two chapters drawing on theory and studies
Ch. 2 Revenue management in the [...] industry
Ch. 3 Revenue management culture
Concludes with adapted model and need for primary research

Thanks to Benjamin Preece (student, Business and Hospitality) for his kind permission to refer to his work.

Methodology
Why primary research? The argument
– How (exactly) data will be collected
– Outline of research process
– Ethics

Findings and discussion
Results of internet survey and interviews:
Theme 1
Theme 2
Theme 3
Theme 4
Charts and short verbatim extracts + analysis
and discussion with reference to literature

Conclusions and recommendations
6.1 Conclusions
   – + limitations
6.2 Recommendations
   – for the industry
   – for future research

Appendices
– Analysis of research methods + reasons for
   inclusion/exclusion
– Interview questions
– Ethical review form
– Survey questions
– Interview transcript

Dissertation 6: Business (hospitality)

Title: *Strategically green: implementing Corporate Social Responsibility in the hospitality and tourism industries*

Abstract:
Purpose
Methodology
Findings
Research limitations
Practical implications
Value
Keywords

Introduction
1.1 Introduction to topic area
1.2 Rationale
1.3 Aim and objectives
Methodology
Chapter structure

Contents

Abstract

Chapter 1 Introduction

Chapter 2 Lit review 1: theory

Chapter 3 Lit review 2: framework
for analysis

Chapter 4 Analysis and discussion

Chapter 5 Conclusions

References

Thanks to Alice Ogle (Business and Hospitality student) for her kind permission to refer to her work.

Lit review 1: theory
2.1 Overview of chapter
2.2 Stakeholders and CSR
2.3 Legitimacy and CSR
2.4 Greenwashing
2.5 Conclusion

Lit review 2:
3.1 Introduction
3.2 Strategic management process
3.3 Models of strategic management, and new model
3.4 Conclusion

Analysis and discussion
4.1 Introduction
4.2 Implementation process for CSR ...
4.3 Analysis of implementation in international hotel chains
Discussion of findings

Conclusions
5.1 Conclusions: review of outcomes of chapters and restatement of aims
5.2 Key findings (bulleted)
5.3 Limitations and directions for future research
Recommendations for the industry

Dissertation 7: Education

An inquiry proposed by a workplace.

The opportunity for this type of inquiry may arise from:

- working in the industry
- several periods in the same workplace (such as *school experience*, or *placement*), or
- work-based study such as a foundation degree.

Abstract
Context of workplace and issue
Aim
How the study was done
What was found
Conclusions and implications for workplace practice

Introduction
Why this topic?
– personal interest/opportunity
Outline of workplace priorities
– need for better understanding of specific issue
Research question and objectives
Overview of chapters

Amina (student, Education).

Title: *Ways to play: how does a children's centre support hard-to-reach parents in playing with their child?*

Contents

Literature review
Overview of chapter
2.1 The problem (as identified in the literature)
2.2 Area 1 [the importance of play]
2.3 Area 2 [the importance of adults/parents in ...]
2.4 Area 3 [why do some parents have difficulty with ...]
2.5 Conclusion
Themes emerging from the literature
Restatement of aim

Methodology
Overview of chapter
3.1 Research approach
3.2 Selection of methods
3.3 Data collection (including ethics)
3.4 Data analysis
3.5 Validity and reliability
(limitations: of the methods, what didn't go to plan, practical constraints)

Results
Overview of chapter: identifying four themes
Results presented by theme in charts, tables, coded observations, extracts from interviews.
Conclusion

Discussion
Overview of chapter
Section headings: themes 1–4 (from Ch. 4). Discussion links results to themes identified in the literature (Ch. 2)

Conclusions
What was learnt?
– link to aim
– reflections
Implications for
– practice, for consideration by the setting

Appendices
– Letter of invitation
– Interview outline
– Transcripts
– Details of observations
– Ethical consent/approval

Dissertation 8: Development studies

A case study

In this case study, Robbie studied a situation from several theoretical angles, and then selected the methods for his primary research to gain a better understanding of the whole.

Title: *The political ecology of HIV/AIDS in the Eastern Cape, South Africa*

Abstract

Introduction
Argument for the study
[The problem/the problem with established
approaches/emerging theoretical approaches/my
case study]
Aim
Chapter outline

Contents

Thanks to Robbie Georgiou (student, Geography and Development Studies) for his kind permission to refer to his work.

Literature review

2.1 Context/situation [HIV/AIDS in a resource-poor context]

2.2 Theoretical approach 1 [Political ecology]

2.3 Theoretical approach 2 [Social capital]

Conclusion: argument for using these approaches for a better understanding of ... [how to increase the community's resilience to HIV/AIDS]

Research questions and methodology

3.1 Aim and objectives

3.2 Focus groups and interviews

3.3 Individual experiences of [living with HIV]

3.4 Participant observation

3.5 Photographic evidence

3.6 Evaluation of methods

Findings from case study organised by theme in a discussion linked to literature from Ch. 2:

4.1 Food security and HIV

4.2 Roles of government policy

4.3 Importance of gender equality

4.4 Fostering resilience by building social capital

Conclusions

− Summary of the argument

− Reiteration of the aim and value of the study

− Key findings

− Suggestions for future research (theoretical and practical)

Theory-based dissertations

Dissertations 9 and 10 are theory-led inquiries. They present their analysis in themed chapters – a different structure to the Findings/Discussion format of dissertations that include a first-hand primary or practical element.

A theoretical study aims to develop or in some small way change the way we see or understand something. This use of theory proposes new ways of understanding a problem, and may also have practical implications. You bring your own question to existing theories and the subject literature to create new insights.

Dissertation 9: Business (hospitality)

Title: *Dining out for distinction*

Abstract
– Aim, context and broad
  approach
– Key theories/theorist and
  relation to topic (dining-out
  practices)
– Location of specific focus
  (dining out) to broader
  social change

Introduction
1.1 Introduction to topic area
1.2 Rationale
1.3 Research aim and objectives
1.4 Methodology/approach
1.5 Chapter structure

Three themed chapters
2 The sociological constructs
  of taste
3 Postmodern food behaviours
4 Contemporary dining out
  cultures
*Each themed chapter has its
own conclusion.*

Conclusion
5.1 Draws the chapter
    conclusions together
– shows the author's position
– concludes her argument: the
  [major theorist's] analysis
  is valid today – but other
  factors are in play ...
5.2 Recommendation:
– future research [social
  theory can lead to better-
  informed practices]

Thanks to Jessica Barwell (Business and Hospitality student) for her kind
permission to refer to her work.

Dissertation 10: Politics and international relations

Title: *The impact of neoliberalism in India: whose growth?*

Abstract
- Aim
- Research questions (2)
- Theoretical approaches
- Argument
- Conclusions

Introduction
- Focus of study
- Key concepts [neoliberalism and inequality]
  Research question 1
- Key theorist [Gramsci]
  Research question 2
- Outline of argument and chapters

Literature review
- Overview
- Role of theory
- Outline and critique of theory [neoliberalism]
- Outline and critique of theorist [Gramsci]
- Conclusion

Contents

Abstract
1 Introduction
2 Literature review
3 ⎫
4 ⎬ Themed analytical
5 ⎭ chapters
6 Conclusion

Themed analytical chapters
Each with brief introduction to argument, and conclusion
3 Historical overview
4 The effects of neoliberalism [Analysis of impact on class, rural poor, employment, production]
5 Study of the state of Kerala [Gramscian analysis]

Conclusion
- Restatement of argument
- Summary by chapter
- Conclusion and implications for development

Thanks to Gaia Pagliara for her kind permission to refer to her Masters dissertation.

Themed analytical chapters are used in these subjects, drawing on primary sources (documents, artefacts, illustrations, photos).

Dissertation 11: History

Title: *Kalymnos, Sponge-Trade and Global History: how a small and remote island connected places on an economic, intellectual and cultural level through its sponge-industry*

Aim and argument
Despite being a remote and tiny island, Kalymnos assumed a leading role in world trade during this period, an issue which is usually overlooked …

Theoretical approach
Approach (or combination of approaches) taken and why (drawing on global history/micro history/local history approaches)

Contents
1 Introduction
  – focus of study
  – importance of the study
  – aims
  – theoretical approach
  – methodology

2
3 } Themed
4 } content
5 } chapters

6 Conclusion

Appendices

Bibliography

Thanks to Vera Pratikaki (student, History) for her kind permission to refer to her work.

Methodology
Why these methods were chosen (a range of
historical sources: artefacts, photos, documents)
to link to **specific aim**
['to view the sponge-industry with a different
lens aiming to identify its significance in an
international context']

Themed (analytical) chapters
2 Introduction to the topic and era [Continuity
   and change]
3 Theme 1: Connections on the economic level
4 Theme 2: Connections on the intellectual
   level
5 Theme 3: Connections on the cultural level

Appendices
Photos

Conclusion
− Key findings
− How the study met your aims
− Why it matters
− Successes and limitations

Bibliography including:
manuscripts, printed primary sources, videos,
secondary sources

Creative arts

Creativity lies at the core of these subjects: music/art/design/dance/film/fashion/media. This is reflected in the choice you are likely to be offered in the balance between the practical and theoretical components that together make up your dissertation.

In a 100% written dissertation, the form may have elements of:

▶ Dissertation 11: themed chapters
▶ Dissertation 3: integrated design and critique
▶ Dissertation 8: theory and case study.

Look at these for ideas you can adapt and apply. The creative arts also have an additional option – to present your practical work as an integral part of your research project, with choice about weighting.

In consultation with your supervisor, you will have to decide on the balance between theory and practice that best suits you and how you want to communicate your research process and outcomes. Bring your ideas to your supervisor – their support and advice will be crucial throughout your dissertation period.

Your decision about this balance needs to be made early on as it will influence both your research process and your production. In all models, the practical work will be expected to illustrate, test or explore the thinking in the written research.

Your options may look something like this:

Written	Practical	May include …
100	0	Theoretical exploration/case study or event write up and critical analysis/illustrations/annotations + commentary
50	50	Performance, live work, website, lecture-recital (music), lecture-demonstration (dance), composition (music), screen work, event, display, exhibition, object, installation, portfolio
25	75	*Linked to …*
75	25	A critical/analytical commentary showing the relationship between practice, theory and thinking
0	100	Usually an exceptional option only if agreed with your supervisor early on. Likely to include a 'viva' or interview in which you explain your process, thinking and research methods

Do the sums – the word count of the written component should reflect the percentage weighting it carries. Knowing what you are aiming for will help you see the shape of the project ahead and where to concentrate your energies.

Dissertation 12: Dance

50% written/50% practical

Whatever the divide between written and practical, the written component will include some form of critical commentary: either on the overall practical component or on a specific section or theme. A close link between the practical and the written analysis may give you a clearer focus.

Once your research is under way, ask yourself:

How am I going to present my research findings?
And **why** is this the best way?

The answer to these questions will become the rationale for your research.

The diagram below shows three options for structuring your dissertation: 100% written (in the middle) and two 50/50 options.

In the **50/50 single idea** option, the written analysis and choreography are linked throughout. In the **50/50 lecture-demonstration**, the 'lec-dem' takes the place of a chapter (here Ch. 2) and the theoretical aspects are developed in the written analysis in the other chapters.

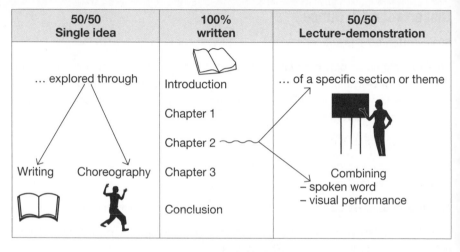

50/50 Single idea	100% written	50/50 Lecture-demonstration
... explored through Writing Choreography	Introduction Chapter 1 Chapter 2 Chapter 3 Conclusion	... of a specific section or theme Combining – spoken word – visual performance

Be prepared to explain your decisions and to discuss them with your supervisor.

Many thanks to Dr Clare Parfitt, Reader in Popular Dance, University of Chichester, UK, for her valuable advice underpinning this section, and for her kind permission to adapt images from her course materials.

What will be in your dissertation?

In Part 5 you have seen some of the many ways of organising your inquiry and structuring your dissertation or research project. These completed dissertations are polished products, each one the outcome of drafting, redrafting, getting it wrong, getting it right, reflecting the decisions the writer made at every turn.

It's your turn now to work out how your dissertation will be. One thing you can be sure – there is no one-size-fits-all magic formula. Your dissertation will reflect your own inquiry and be shaped by your own hard work and the decisions you make along the way.

In writing your dissertation, you are not simply writing *about* something, but taking your reader with you on your journey of discovery – through your argument.

Part 6 focuses on writing: it shows how to ensure your writing is well-structured, persuasive and that your 'voice' comes through in an appropriate way.

6
WRITING AND
ARGUMENT

WRITING PARAGRAPHS

LANGUAGE

I THINK

USING 'I'

ARGUMENT &

Paragraphs are important: here's why[6]

Paragraphs have a *structure*

- A paragraph develops **one main idea**.
- This main idea is usually expressed clearly in one sentence – the first, or **topic, sentence**.
- Paragraphs have a beginning, a middle and an end. The sentences in the middle explain, develop, evidence or modify the main idea in the topic sentence. The last sentence often returns to the idea in the topic sentence to show how it has developed.

Paragraph structure has a *purpose*

It makes it easier to

- **Read**: the main idea is first, and you know that this idea will be developed before you move on.

---

6 Many of the approaches here have developed from previous publications. See *Getting critical* Ch. 11 in this series.

- ▶ **Plan**: each paragraph develops a single point. You can plan by mapping out the points.
- ▶ **Write**: new point, new paragraph. Start each paragraph with a clear statement of the point you are making, then add detail.

How to write a paragraph

To write a paragraph, start with an idea of what you want to say, a point you want to put across. Through the paragraph develop this idea into a short block of text, and your section builds up – paragraph by paragraph.

A paragraph plan

1 **Start with the topic sentence** to express the main idea.
2 **Explain or define any abstract, key or problematic terms** to clarify the topic sentence.
3 **Show your evidence** to support your main idea or argument in the topic sentence.
4 **Comment on the evidence** to show how it supports or develops the main idea. If appropriate, mention other evidence (examples, studies, experiments, interpretations) to widen the discussion.
5 **Conclude**. Look back to your topic sentence and ask yourself:
   ▶ How have I moved on/developed the main idea in it?
   ▶ Where am I going next?
   ▶ Then write the last sentence.

This basic structure can also be used for more sophisticated writing.

Workshop 9: Paragraph planning

Below is a paragraph from the literature review of a Masters dissertation. How does it match the paragraph plan? Try adding the numbers of the paragraph plan to the text.

In politically unstable countries the roles of stakeholders may be different to those in developed or developing countries (Petridis 2005; Mansfeld and Hong 2009). Stakeholders are also likely to have a different profile and priorities to those in more stable countries. In less stable countries the private sector is likely to play a key role in pressurising the government to allocate time and money for tourism development. However, as Mehlim (2016) points out, the government may regard tourism planning as a low priority in the context of the political situation in the country. He acknowledges that while not-for-profit organisations and other professionals may play an important role in other respects, the government may not be responsive to their efforts in relation to tourism planning. In these circumstances, Czepiel (2014) argues that the private sector can become the driver in tourism planning in politically unstable countries. It can draw together the different groups to form a persuasive group of stakeholders, prepared to seize the opportunity to position past or even current conflicts as tourist attractions.

Kiran (student, Business and Tourism).

Turn the following page upside down to see how the paragraph has been planned:

In politically unstable countries the roles of stakeholders may be different to those in developed or developing countries (Petridis 2005; Mansfeld and Hong 2009).[1] Stakeholders are also likely to have a different profile and priorities to those in more stable countries.[2] In less stable countries the private sector is likely to play a key role in pressurising the government to allocate time and money for tourism development.[3] However, as Mehlim (2016) points out, the government may regard tourism planning as a low priority in the context of the political situation in the country. He acknowledges that while not-for-profit organisations and other professionals may play an important role in other respects, the government may not be responsive to their efforts in relation to tourism planning. In these circumstances, Czepiel (2014) argues that the private sector can become the driver in tourism planning in politically unstable countries.[3/4] It can draw together the different groups to form a persuasive group of stakeholders, prepared to seize the opportunity to position past or even current conflicts as tourist attractions.[4/5]

1 Topic sentence

2 Explain/define

3 Move to supporting evidence

3/4 Supporting evidence, discussion and argument intertwined showing the position of the writer

4/5 Comment, conclusion and look ahead to next paragraph

This paragraph is persuasive – and draws the reader to the writer's bold concluding point. By the time you reach the end, you realise that this is where the writer was going to from the first sentence. You have been carried there through a subtle blend of argument and evidence. How does it work?

A paragraph is, in effect, a unit of argument. Each paragraph builds on the one that went before, and leads to the one that comes after. In this way you develop a persuasive argument in a logical and coherent way.

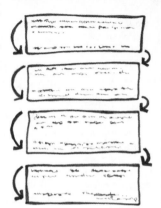

The language of argument

This chapter takes a closer look at how the writer of the paragraph above progresses his argument through choice of language – at how the 'moves' of a paragraph are intertwined with the sources the writer draws on.

Argument:
A connected series of statements intended to establish (or subvert) a position; a process of reasoning.
Shorter Oxford Dictionary

The writer does not comment directly on the sources he uses. Nevertheless, the point he is making and the direction of his argument are perfectly clear to the reader: he has a clear 'voice'. This invisible current is what is meant by having a 'position' or line of reasoning. You are providing the 'golden thread' to take the reader from where they are when they start reading your work, through to where you want them to be – on your terrain.

Let's take a closer look at how it works:

For more on 'voice' see *Where's your argument?* (2016) in this series.

Tracing the 'golden thread of argument'	
In politically unstable countries the roles of stakeholders may be different to those in developed or developing countries (Petridis 2005; Mansfeld and Hong 2009).[1]	**1 Topic sentence** Sets out the argument – and engages the reader: *how will this writer progress this idea of the 'different' role of stakeholders in these countries?*
Stakeholders are also likely to have a different profile and priorities to those in more stable countries.[2]	**2 Explain/define** The reader wants to see the writer is in control and can propose a sensible focus for the analysis and argument to follow: *differences narrowed to 'role' and 'priorities'.*
In less stable countries the private sector is likely to play a key role in pressurising the government to allocate time and money for tourism development.[3] However, as Mehlim (2016) points out, the government may regard tourism planning as a low priority in the context of the	**3 Move to supporting evidence** Careful steer by the writer to focus the reader on the key point of the discussion: *how to draw the government into supporting tourism.* The argument is set up.

political situation in the country. He acknowledges that while not-for-profit organisations and other professionals may play an important role in other respects, the government may not be responsive to their efforts in relation to tourism planning. In these circumstances, Czepiel (2014) argues that the private sector can become the driver in tourism planning in politically unstable countries.[3/4]	**3/4 Evidence** and **argument** intertwined – showing the writer's awareness of the debates in the field and the **position** in relation to them. *Comment is implicit through the choice and sequence of studies referred to. Note the impact of the verbs: points out/ acknowledges/argues.* *A new voice – by referring to Czepiel at this point, the writer takes the next step in his argument as the lead-in to his conclusion.*
It can draw together the different groups to form a persuasive group of stakeholders, prepared to seize the opportunity to position past or even current conflicts as tourist attractions [4/5]	**4/5 Comment, conclusion** and **look ahead** to next paragraph. Returning to the argument of the topic sentence: *the word 'persuasive' to describe the stakeholders shows the writer's position, drawing the reader onto the writer's ground.*

The conclusion shows the distance the writer has travelled from the topic sentence, and as readers we have followed his line of reasoning. We are ready now for the next paragraph, where he has the opportunity to convince us – or not – of the validity of his proposition.

Words that help argument

You saw from the paragraph above how carefully the writer picks his way through the research. The language he uses helps to position himself in relation to the writers whose work he draws on:

> *As Mehlim (2016) points out …*
> *Czepiel (2013) argues …*

And where the writer had no need or wish to go into the detail of a source in a general point, he tells the reader where to go for the evidence: *… (Petridis 2005; Mansfeld and Hong 2009).*

Careful choice of verbs shows your voice. You can signal doubt ('claims'), caution ('suggests'), specific interest ('points out') and so on. This is a fundamental skill in conveying your argument and will lift your writing from being merely 'descriptive' to being analytical and evaluative.

See how it's done:

Six magic verbs		
Smith (2018)	*points out* *argues* *maintains* *claims* *concludes* *suggests*	... that preventative medicine is far more cost effective, and therefore better adapted to the developing world.

University of Manchester (2018).

Using these words effectively gives your reader a clear insight into what you think about what you read – and this of course is what your dissertation supervisor wants to see. It works something like this. As they read, the tutor will be thinking …

Tutor
What does this tell me about what my student thinks about …?

The student writes	The tutor thinks ...
Smith (2018) ...	
points out that ...	*Ah! This student has picked out something interesting ... they have read thoughtfully.*
argues that ...	*They've done some sustained reading and can follow Smith's line of reasoning ...*
maintains that ...	*I feel a 'but' coming ... This student is keeping a bit of distance here. Interesting research but ...?*
claims that ...	*My student is being careful here. Either it's emerging research, or they aren't convinced by it.*
concludes that ...	*My student is picking the key point of the research, a useful takeaway point ...*
suggests that ...	*A mature and balanced way of presenting a perspective ...*

Six magic words? Yes, they are, and there are plenty more words like these to choose from. They lift your writing and open up a conversation with your reader. And that is exactly what you want to achieve.

Writing isn't a cruise around the islands!

This is a cop-out by the tour guide! You want more than a patchwork of snippets from other tour guides.

Your reader wants more too: from introduction to conclusion, via lit review, methodology and discussion, your reader is looking for the 'value-added' from you. When you are positioning yourself in relation to the different authors you have read, your reader wants to hear your voice: where are YOU in all this? The *So what? What next?* questions:

> *Well, is it the biggest? And why are you telling me?*

> *So what if it's volcanic? What difference does that make?*

> *Why this boring quote about tourists?*

This is the 'descriptive' writing tutors really don't want … and I hope that now you can see why!

Four words to ruin your writing

~~*Said …*~~   ~~*States …*~~   ~~*Highlights …*~~   ~~*Looks at …*~~

All this tells me as a reader is that you have read the source (probably) but you have absolutely nothing to say about it!

'States' does have one important use: to report on a key point from an authoritative source (eg government policy or report, industry standards, professional practice guidelines) before you move on to discuss it. For example:

> Ofsted **states** that early years education has 'never been stronger' (2015, p. 6). However, Hartman (2017) **points out** that …

You report directly and neutrally …

… before commenting on different views, and showing your own position through how you refer to your sources

Source: Ofsted (2015). Early years annual report. Available at www.gov.uk/government/uploads/system/uploads/attachment_data/file/445730/Early_years_report_2015.pdf (Accessed 12 February 2018).

How visible do you want to be in your writing?

This depends on the research traditions of your subject area and what you decide or are expected to do. In some subjects (science subjects for example) the focus is on the process, not on the researcher/writer, so the writing style avoids 'I'. In others (some social sciences and humanities) the researcher is more visible as part of the process, and the selective use of 'I' is appropriate.[7]

Check with your supervisor early on. Does your supervisor agree with the points below? Always follow their advice!

Reflections

If you are asked to include reflections (for example, on what prompted your interest in your research area, or how you would use your findings in your practice), use 'I':

---

7 See *Reflective writing* in this series for advice on writing style.

- *My interest in the subject arose when …*
- *I was offered the opportunity to …*
- *By doing this study I can say now that my practice is supported by evidence …*

Introducing and concluding chapters

It is good practice to introduce and conclude each chapter (briefly) to signpost your reader through your work. Decide on the style for this:

Visible author: using 'I'	Less visible author style
In this chapter I explain the process I followed …	*This section of the study will examine …*

Or you can move between both styles:

Visible author: using 'I'	Less visible author style
I draw on the theoretical approaches of …	*Chapter 2 reviews the literature on …*
I draw on primary qualitative data … then put forward the case for …	*This section presents the aim and objectives of … It then puts forward …*

In your methodology

This is where you set out what you did: you have to make judgements about how visible you are in your account, especially in primary research.

Visible author: using 'I'	Less visible author style
All the papers I identified were …	*Subjects were asked to …*
By situating myself within the treatment community I was in a position to …	*The survey was developed by using …*
I felt it was not appropriate to conduct research in this way …	*The questionnaire was devised with the help of …*

Difficulties arise when students try to record their actions in detail, or are asked to include reflections but *not* to use 'I'. This can produce clunky and awkward writing:

Try not to write like this!
… the restricted timeframe forced the author to …
The research process gave the researcher invaluable experience in …
The author completed an electronic database search …

Part 6 has outlined some core writing skills and decisions you will draw on as you write up your research. These are not decisions you make once: like everything else in research, it is an iterative process – you go backwards and forwards – and though it may not always seem like it, you do move on.

If you get stuck, take a break. Do something active. When you go back to it with your brain refreshed, something may just click.

Part 7 is about the endgame. With all your major chapters drafted, they now need to be transformed into a polished and persuasive document.

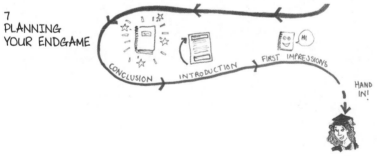

7
PLANNING
YOUR ENDGAME

CONCLUSION → INTRODUCTION → FIRST IMPRESSIONS

HI

HAND
IN!

As **researcher**, your job is pretty much done. As **writer**, you still have work to do: writing your conclusion, introduction and abstract. As **project manager** and **editor**, you take control, bringing all the strands of your dissertation together to that wonderful moment when you hand in the printed and bound document.

Submit an electronic copy via Feedback Studio (Turnitin) AND TWO printed copies by 16.00 on Friday Week 8.

Time planning!
Skim through Part 7 quickly and write down how long you think you need to allow to hand-in.

....

LONDON 4:00

Be clear about what you are aiming for

Remind yourself what a good completed dissertation looks like. Part 5 gives you a flavour, but the real thing is better.

Your assessors will approach your dissertation rather like you look at others. You are in a hurry and anything unclear will annoy you. You use the structure to guide you: a dissertation has a beginning, middle and end. So does each chapter, section and paragraph. You want to see something like this:

Dissertation	Chapter	Section	Paragraph
1 **Introduction**	**Chapter 2: xxxx** Introduction – this chapter ...	**2.2 xxxxx xx xxxx** Introduction/link	The five times more to attract new customers that it does to keep an existing customer happy. Conversely it needs to be considered that even within a customer base not all patrons will be profitable to the company. In retail banking for example, the This definition covers the important point that the needs and objectives of both the customer and the organisation must be satisfied. Satisfying customers should be an essential part of marketing activity for it is cheaper to satisfy and thereby retain existing customers than it is to obtain new ones (Oliver 2015). According to Masterson st al (2016) it costs approximately five times more to attract new customers that it does to keep an existing customer happy. Conversely it needs to be considered that even within a customer base not all patrons will be profitable to the company. In retail banking for example, the existing customer happy. Conversely it needs to be considered that even within a customer base not all patrons will be profitable to the company.
2	2.1		
	2.2		
3			
4			
5	2.3		
6 **Conclusion**	**Conclusion**	**Conclusion**/link	

Structure helps the reader locate whatever they are reading within the whole: the writer promises at the beginning, and delivers at the end. It makes for a happy reader!

What are the examiners looking for?

Check your guidance and make sure you understand what it means: ask if in doubt. Whether set out formally or not, assessors will be looking for evidence of what you have learnt (learning outcomes) and will be assessing your work against assessment criteria – something like this:

Overall, your readers will be looking for

Strong internal consistency making the research project a convincing whole, clearly addressing the research question in:

▶ Argument
▶ Logical structure
▶ Use of evidence (primary/secondary) to support argument
▶ Critical and reflective awareness of strengths and limitations
▶ Clear conclusions and recommendations

Specifically, this will show in your

▶ *Research question*: problem or investigation: clear aim, objectives, focus, convincing rationale
▶ *Literature review*: range of reading; grasp of theoretical principles and applications; relevance to research question; independent research; depth of knowledge and understanding
▶ *Research methods*: appreciation of methodological issues; rationale for approach chosen; systematic information/data gathering and analysis; critical awareness of strengths and limitations
▶ *Findings*: presentation of data and analysis; identification of themes
▶ *Synthesis*: bringing together research to show you've grasped the relationship between them
▶ *Presentation*: consistent structure; no errors or typos; appropriate writing style (including integration of citations); correct referencing

With thanks to Cathy Burgess, Faculty of Business (Oxford Brookes University), for her kind permission to include the above. Adapted and with additions from Science, Education and Health and Social Care.

The key point is that the dissertation should be a *convincing whole* with a logic and argument that runs from start to finish.

Drafting and redrafting 1: your main chapters	
You've been focusing on getting the ideas and information down. Now look at the whole and be prepared to rearrange and prune.	**Edit it** for the big picture: • Check content, structure, balance. • Introduce and conclude each chapter/section to show your argument. • Leave enough word count for your introduction and conclusion chapters.

Take special care to back up while you are editing and cutting and pasting between versions.

These two chapters are key in crafting your dissertation – and in the impression you make on your reader.

▶ The introduction is written or revised *last*, when you know exactly what you are introducing.
▶ Write the conclusion after all the other chapters – *before* you write the introduction.

In this way, you know that your promise of what lies ahead (in the introduction) is indeed fulfilled (in the conclusion). Equally, you can be sure that the point you arrived at in your conclusion is indeed a logical progression from the introduction.

Writing your conclusion

In the conclusion you **look back** at the whole dissertation journey and set out the takeaway points. You also **look forward** to show why your findings matter, how your research relates to the issues you identified in choosing your topic and in working out your research question. You suggest how your findings might be used or implemented in, for example, your workplace or industry.

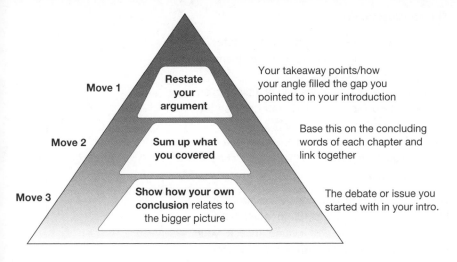

Move 1 — **Restate your argument** — Your takeaway points/how your angle filled the gap you pointed to in your introduction

Move 2 — **Sum up what you covered** — Base this on the concluding words of each chapter and link together

Move 3 — **Show how your own conclusion** relates to the bigger picture — The debate or issue you started with in your intro.

Your reader will look at your conclusions before they read the whole. Do articulate clearly what you have achieved and learnt. It will motivate your reader to trace the process through your dissertation.

The conclusion:

▶ is usually a short, free-standing chapter. It may be longer in a dissertation with thematic chapters in the body.

▶ is sometimes placed at the end of a discussion chapter (see Dissertation 2). You can use the same structure for this section.

▶ contains no new material. If you think of a last-minute addition, place it in the relevant chapter – or leave it out.

Below are elements of a conclusion which may be used as subheadings or in combinations. Consider which you will include (check your guidance) and the order in which you place them.

What's in your conclusion?	Yes? No?
Restatement of aim, or **problem** you addressed	
What you learnt: key findings	
Limitations of your research What you didn't do, couldn't do; the limits of your data, methods or circumstances	
Implications for – practice – policy – personal learning	
Areas for further research – where your research might go next – unanswered questions/future research	
Recommendations If appropriate (see Dissertations 4, 5, 6, 7, 9)	
Reflections on personal learning If explicitly required. Write in a 'reflective' style, using 'I'	

Writing your introduction

This section is about that part of the introductory chapter where you:

 ▶ introduce your reader to your topic
 ▶ interest them in what you have to say – your argument
 ▶ lead them to your aims.

By the end, you want your reader to be saying, *'Yeah! Go for it! I quite see why you want to research this, and I really want to see what you find ...'*

Write your introduction straight after you've written your conclusion, setting aside any earlier versions. This is how you make sure that your conclusion and introduction are joined at the hip!

Think of your introduction as a series of moves:

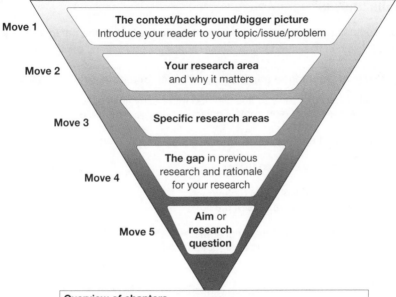

Move 1 — The context/background/bigger picture
Introduce your reader to your topic/issue/problem

Move 2 — Your research area
and why it matters

Move 3 — Specific research areas

Move 4 — The gap in previous research and rationale for your research

Move 5 — Aim or research question

Overview of chapters
Use this to show progression and linking, so it's more than just Ch. 2 does this, Ch. 3 does that. This is your reader's road map.

Using the 'moves'

The topic sentence of each paragraph indicates the content of the paragraph – and shows the moves. In this introduction, some moves include several paragraphs.

The effects of listening to music on people with dementia	Moves
Dementia is a broad term ... It is claimed that nearly all people with dementia will develop some significant behavioural problems ...	Move 1
...	
Agitated and aggressive behaviours are frequently thought of as ...	Move 2
The use of medication to manage ...	
...	
Non-pharmacological techniques ...	Move 3
The soothing effects of music ...	
...	
However the quality of some of the research [...] has been questioned ...	Move 4
leading to ...	
Why my research is needed to fill the gap! And the aim of my research ...	Move 5

Vidya (Adult nursing)

Workshop 10: Your introduction in five moves

→ Draw yourself a large inverted triangle.
→ Number the moves from 1 to 5.
→ Write a single topic sentence for each move. You may decide to start with Move 5, the aim.
→ Read the five sentences out loud to yourself.

You can then develop each move into a couple of sentences – and see the shape of your introduction emerging.

Your introductory chapter may also include additional elements (see the dissertation outlines in Part 5). These include:

- methodology (Dissertations 6, 9, 11)
- literature review leading to aims, especially in science subjects (Dissertation 1)
- hypothesis (linked to aims)
- preliminary literature review (Dissertation 4)
- your personal or practice reasons for choosing this topic to research (Dissertations 4, 7)
- scope and limitations (Dissertations 5, 6).

Drafting and redrafting 2: add conclusion and introduction

Make sure you promise (in the introduction) what you deliver (in the conclusion) and that they reflect any shift in focus that happened along the way.

Edit it to make sure the points come across clearly: flow, linking, logic, topic sentences; references; word count.

Check the appearance of your pages: indentations, spaces between paragraphs and sections.

Look at your pages upside down – you will see the visual impact without the distraction of reading it.

Can you see the golden thread of argument running from start to finish?

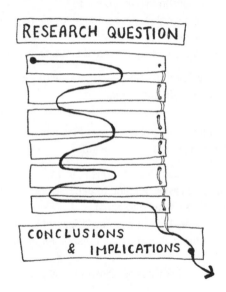

RESEARCH QUESTION

CONCLUSIONS & IMPLICATIONS

Become an editor!

Finally! Take off your writing hat and become an editor. Leave at least a day since when you last looked at it so you come at it cold and see what's really there (not what you *think* is there).

Be organised about version control. Date the footer and file name of each version, and back it up!

Drafting and redrafting 3: is looking good	
Add Contents, Lists of Tables, Figures, Acknowledgements, Abstract, Appendices. Then sit down for a good (but critical) read …	**Proofread** for anything that doesn't make sense or sound right; write short sentences. Check for spelling, punctuation, grammar, part sentences, typos, lookalike words popped in by the computer, anything with a wiggly line.

Watch out for:

- Too many or too long quotes: shorten them to 'keywords', or summarise (keeping the reference).
- Funny-sounding phrases where you cut and pasted.
- Tenses, especially bits from earlier drafts of your methodology. This is now 'what you DID' (past tense), not what you planned to do (future).
- Check your references. Every source in the text should be listed in the references and every listing should be there in the text. Follow the recommended style meticulously.
- Anything that especially annoys your supervisor (check previously marked work).
- Your favourite errors!

Does it make sense?

If it doesn't make sense to you, it won't make sense to anyone else! Try reading it out loud, or ask a friend or family member to read it.

When you hand it in, your dissertation will be transformed: gift-wrapped in its shiny cover with pages that flick like a book, it will be ready for the reader. Your supervisor – supporter, mentor, guide – will pick it up as assessor and examiner and turn the pages. What will they see?

Title page

Check you meet the formal requirements of your title page, and any additional required wording or pages, such as statement of originality.

Acknowledgements

Thank everyone who helped or supported you, with an indication of how they helped:

▶ your supervisor by name (a MUST!)
▶ anyone else who inspired you in some way
▶ participants/subjects
▶ people who offered practical help
▶ friends and family.

But maintain confidentiality/anonymity here too!

And my thanks to Mrs Pugwash, headteacher of Pudsey School, and Class 2 teacher Mrs Flitworth, and those lovely children, Mehmet, Emmie, Caz, Rodrigo, Leon, Annie ... WHOOPS!!

Abstract

You've read a lot of these, remember? Check the abstracts of dissertations you have access to, articles in your subject area and look at the dissertations in Part 5.

An abstract consists of four short paragraphs (often run together) summarising your research.

1 **Aim** or **research question**: why the research was needed.
2 **How** you did it.
3 **What** you found/what your research shows or suggests.
4 **Conclusions**: the takeaway points. Recommendations if appropriate.

Keep it clear and short. But do work on it – it is your shop window.

Contents

Your reader will want to get an overview of the structure, organisation and coherence of your dissertation.

Bald chapter headings are not enough:

Chapter 1: Introduction
Chapter 2: Literature review
Chapter 3: Methodology
Chapter 4: …

But don't drown them in detail:

> **2. Literature review**
>
> 2.1 xxxxxxxx
>> 2.1.1 xxxx xxxxxxx
>>> 2.1.1.1 xxxxx
>>> 2.1.1.2 xxxxxx
>>> 2.1.1.3 xxxxxxxx
>> 2.1.2 xxxxxx xxxxxxxxx

Give enough detail to show the relationship between topics in the chapter:

> **Chapter 2: Greenwashing? The role of stakeholders and concept of legitimacy**
>
> 2.1 Overview of chapter
> 2.2 Stakeholders and CSR
> 2.3 The role of legitimacy and CSR
> 2.4 Greenwashing
> 2.5 Conclusion

Lists of tables, figures, illustrations

These give an indication of the detail of your work and the thoroughness of your research.

And at the end …

References

These come immediately at the end of your text. (In Humanities the 'Bibliography' is usually placed last, after any Appendices and Acknowledgements – see Dissertation 11.)

Appendices (where used)

These are not a dumping ground for anything you can't fit into your word count! They are material your reader may wish to refer to in order to see the sources for the points you discuss in your text.

For example, in your text:

… a list of questions was developed from noting gaps in the literature (see Appendix 2) …
… the University Code of Practice (see Appendix 4) was …

See also *Referencing and understanding plagiarism* (2017) in this series.

Appendices might include:

- raw data or summary tables of primary research results
- data collection tools used: eg questionnaire, prompt questions for interviews, interview transcript, photos, observation records, record sheets
- analytical tools: eg CASP (in Health and Social Care), measurement tools, statistical tests
- procedural records: ethical approval letters of permission, participant information sheet, consent form, safety considerations.

Now head off to the Print Room!

Time planning, again!

Do you need to revise how long you need to allow for the final stages?

....

Then there is the unexpected – which, by definition is ...
err ... unexpected!

If you are even 10 minutes late you are awarded ZERO MARKS.

The hand-in moment is the destination of a long journey with many phases. Celebrate your achievement, sleep it off and enjoy the warm glow of achievement.

This long project at the end of your course of study is a major achievement. It will play a part in determining your overall grade: you have demonstrated your ability to become expert in a specific aspect of your studies.

But it's more than that. Gaining deep knowledge and understanding of one area is indicative that you can do the same in other contexts. This will be of interest to a future employer.

You have demonstrated your personal, research and project management skills to:

- ✓ set up your own inquiry
- ✓ work independently
- ✓ carry out research – and become expert!
- ✓ develop a mature and effective working relationship with your supervisor
- ✓ manage the project from start to finish.

This will stand you in good stead in your next steps, whatever they may be.

Good luck – and enjoy!

References

Aveyard H (2014). *Doing a literature review in health and social care: a practical guide*. 3rd edn. Maidenhead: Open University Press.

Cochrane Collaboration (2018). *What is Cochrane evidence and how can it help you?* Available at www.cochrane.org/what-is-cochrane-evidence (Accessed 21 February 2018).

Cooper H and Shoolbred M (2016). *Where's your argument?* London: Palgrave.

Critical Appraisal Skills Programme (CASP) (2017). Available at www.casp-uk.net/

Godfrey J (2014). *Reading and making notes*. 2nd edn. London: Palgrave.

Thomas G (2017). *Doing research.* 2nd edn. London: Palgrave.

Thomas G (2017). *How to do your research project.* 3rd edn. London: Sage.

University of Manchester (2018). *Academic phrasebank*. Available at www.phrasebank.manchester.ac.uk.

Wallace M and Wray A (2011). *Critical reading and writing for postgraduates*. 2nd edn. London: Sage.

Williams K (2014). *Getting critical.* 2nd edn. London: Palgrave.

Williams K and Davies M (2017). *Referencing and understanding plagiarism.* 2nd edn. London: Palgrave.

Williams K and Reid M (2011). *Time management*. Basingstoke: Palgrave Macmillan.

Williams K, Bethell E, Lawton J, Parfitt C, Richardson M, Rowe V (2010). *Planning your PhD.* Basingstoke: Palgrave Macmillan.

Williams K, Bethell E, Lawton J, Parfitt-Brown C, Richardson M, Rowe V (2011). *Completing your PhD.* Basingstoke: Palgrave Macmillan.

Williams K, Woolliams M and Spiro J (2012). *Reflective writing*. Basingstoke: Palgrave Macmillan.

Useful resources

Pears R and Shields G (2016). *Cite them right* (10th edn). London: Palgrave.

This much expanded edition gives models for references for the most used referencing styles. Watch out for the most recent edition. *Cite them right online* is available via many university libraries.

RMIT *Learning Lab*. https://emedia.rmit.edu.au/learninglab/.
From the home page, choose your area: writing skills, study skills, assessment tasks, postgraduate and more. Excellent advice is linked to the writing skills you need – all readily accessible.

University of Manchester (2018). *Academic phrasebank*. www.phrasebank. manchester.ac.uk/.

This superb resource is for anyone looking for words and phrases to use in their writing, especially if you find yourself using only two or three verbs to introduce a source. It is user-friendly and well organised – a must!

Index